"**What Are Spiritual Gifts?** is a careful study of the subject of spiritual gifts. These easy to read, well-constructed sentences make for pleasant and comfortable use by groups or individuals. The "Life Scenarios" and questions after each chapter are thought provoking and provide opportunity for class discussion and interaction. I highly recommend this excellent, thorough, and well-documented study."
—**Reverend Donald Richardson**, former Denominational District Secretary/Treasurer in the New York District

"The information presented in **What Are Spiritual Gifts?** is sorely needed in the local church today. This broad approach to the topic of spiritual gifts is excellent and exciting. Providing facilitators ensures the best method of presentation.
—**Reverend Ed White**, former Senior Pastor, District Men's Ministries Director

"In this study, the author demonstrates both scholarship and objectivity, at times leading the reader to certain inevitable conclusions but also enabling the reader to make sound independent judgments, which may differ to some extent from the judgments of others. The author enriches the work via a number of problem situations, which will keep the reader in touch with life as it really is."
—**Irvin H. Ziemann**, Associate Professor of Biblical Languages Emeritus, Southeastern University

WHAT ARE SPIRITUAL GIFTS?

WHAT ARE SPIRITUAL GIFTS?
How to Decide When Even the Experts Disagree

C. A. PATRICK

MJM

MORNING JOY MEDIA
SPRING CITY, PENNSYLVANIA

Published by Morning Joy Media.

Visit www.morningjoymedia.com for more information on bulk discounts and special promotions, or e-mail your questions to contact@morningjoymedia.com.

Cover Design: Dan Desrosiers
Interior Design: Debbie Capeci

ISBN 978-1-937107-34-5

Printed in the United States of America

Dedication

Dedicated to my mother, Tiny Margaret Wilssens, who embraces the gift of faith; and my father, Joseph Omar Wilssens, who blesses us with his gift of discernment.

Special Thanks

Special thanks to my "study testers" and "editors": Randy, Alicia, Cara, Kaitlin, Dale, Sharon, Tammy, Rick, and Pastor Don; to my son-in-law, Dan, for his work on the cover design; and to my New Testament Greek professor, Prof. Irvin Ziemann, for helping to edit the study in its initial stages, and for being my teacher, mentor, and encourager.

CONTENTS

Lesson One
The Early Church

Introduction

In recent years, much has been written about "spiritual gifts" and their importance in ministry. But what exactly are spiritual gifts and what is their purpose? Theologian Richard B. Gaffin Jr. believes that since around 1960, few topics have received more attention in the worldwide church than the topic of spiritual gifts, and that at times the topic has been the subject of great controversy and division.[1] New Testament scholar Craig Keener believes this controversy has intensified since the charismatic renewal of the 1960s and 1970s.[2]

Why would a subject such as spiritual gifts, which was meant to bring unity to the church, be the cause of so much controversy? What are spiritual gifts? What was their purpose in the early church? And what significance do they have for the church today?

Despite volumes of material that have been written on the subject of spiritual gifts, there continues to be considerable controversy surrounding the subject. Probably the biggest area of disagreement involves a basic definition of what exactly spiritual gifts are. You may have asked or heard other people ask questions such as, "Do my God-given gifts encompass talents and abilities, or are they strictly supernatural enablements given to me after salvation?" "Have some gifts that were previously a part of the New Testament church ceased?" "Are there other gifts beyond those found in Scripture?" If you have asked any of these questions, you are not alone. Unfortunately, even Bible scholars disagree in their answers.

As you read this you may be asking yourself, "How can I come to an understanding of what spiritual gifts are if even the experts disagree?" You might also be wondering whether it is worth the effort of wading through yet another Bible study on this very controversial subject.

Peacemaking is not avoiding conflict. Running from a problem, pretending it doesn't exist, or being afraid to talk about it is actually cowardice.
RICK WARREN

---

1. Richard B. Gaffin Jr., *Perspectives on Pentecost* (Grand Rapids, MI: Baker Book House, 1979), 9.
2. Craig S. Keener, *Gift Giver: The Holy Spirit for Today* (Grand Rapids, MI: Baker Academic, 2001), 91.

First of all, I want to assure you that as the author of this study I am not interested in giving you my personal ideas concerning spiritual gifts. After all, my opinions are no better than the next person's. Instead, what I hope to accomplish is to allow you to come to your own conclusions by guiding you through a study of Scripture, exploring New Testament Greek terminologies, and giving you the resources to interact with the varying ideas of some of the best-known scholars and teachers on the subject. As you work through the lessons and interact with the opinions of others, you will be encouraged to come to your own conclusions and to apply these conclusions to everyday life through the use of real-life scenarios and personal applications. The goal of this Bible study is not to identify your individual giftings (although you may find some of these along the journey) but to come to your own conclusions regarding what spiritual gifts are—their meaning and purpose.

Some of you may be working through these lessons alone and others may be interacting with a small group. Please remember that if you are working with a small group, your ideas might differ from those of others in your group. This is okay. Even if you disagree on the particulars of what spiritual gifts are, I think you will find that, in the end, you will agree on their unified purpose. As you do so, I hope that you will also learn to respect the various opinions of others. Thomas à Kempis, a fifteenth-century theologian, once said, "Who is so wise as to have perfect knowledge of all things?"

The Bible translation used for this study is the *New International Version* (NIV); however any reputable translation is acceptable. Choose a translation that is easy for you to understand. You may even choose to use more than one translation as you study.

God has designed us for ministry by blessing us with special gifts that are unique to each of us. Be assured that this includes you. As we explore the Scriptures, I pray that God will give you revelation as to your importance in His kingdom work.

The Churches at Rome, Corinth, and Ephesus

Although the apostle Paul makes reference to the gifts given to Christians throughout his numerous epistles to the church, his main teachings concerning gifts and their relationship to the body of Christ are included in Romans 12:1–13; 1 Corinthians 12–14; and Ephesians 4:1–16. The most comprehensive

> *My business is not to remake myself, but to make the absolute best of what God made.*
> **ROBERT BROWNING**

CONTENTS

of these passages was written to the Corinthian church in 1 Corinthians 12–14. Although some believe that Paul's list of nine gifts in 1 Corinthians 12:8–10 is a complete list, the similar language used in the other texts lead many Bible scholars to believe otherwise. Each of these passages focuses on the uniqueness of the individual and the importance of their God-given enablements within the body of Christ.

Many keys are available to help us understand Scripture. One helpful method involves a study of the culture and time period in which the message is written. In this lesson, we'll take each of the three passages mentioned above and evaluate their cultural settings. By doing this, we can more accurately understand the people and situation to which the Scripture was addressed. When today's missionaries prepare to go to a foreign country to minister, they prepare by studying the culture and language of the people to which they will be ministering. One of the biggest mistakes missionaries can make is to assume that the people they are trying to reach think and speak in the same way they do. For example, if a missionary is ministering in a developing country and encouraging the people not to *"store up for [themselves] treasures on earth, where moths and vermin destroy, and where thieves break in and steal"* (Matthew 6:19), he or she might do well to avoid using such examples as pursuing risky investments in the stock market or comparing treasures on earth to buying a new sports car.

Paul originally wrote Romans, 1 Corinthians, and Ephesians as letters (epistles) to the New Testament church. In reading any letter, we should keep in mind that the subject matter is very much one-sided. That is, although we can clearly read the communication on the part of the writer, we are only hearing one side of the conversation.

In their book *How to Read the Bible for All Its Worth*, theologians Gordon Fee and Douglas Stuart note that problems represented in Scripture may be difficult to interpret due in part to these one-sided conversations. "We have the answers, but we do not always know what the questions or problems were—or even if there was a problem. It is much like listening to one end of a telephone conversation and trying to figure out who is on the other end and what that unseen party is saying."[3]

No missionary worth his or her salt would enter a field without first doing an exhaustive study of the culture he or she seeks to reach.
GRAHAM JOHNSTON

---

3.   Gordon D. Fee and Douglas Stuart, *How to Read the Bible for All Its Worth* (Grand Rapids, MI: Zondervan, 2003), 58.

Read this letter from a father to his son and answer the following questions.

Dear David,

It has only been two weeks since you left but we already miss you. We are looking forward to seeing you again at Thanksgiving.

I was sorry to hear about the problems you are having with Mark. I know that it must be disappointing for you after all the plans that you made together. I will continue to pray that you will be reconciled. Perhaps it was all a misunderstanding and will be resolved quickly. Remember the words of Proverbs 16:7: "When the Lord takes pleasure in anyone's way, he causes their enemies to make peace with them."

Your mother is doing better, but often has difficulty sleeping. Your letters are an encouragement to her. They are the bright spot of her day. Sheila is enjoying school, although we are not sure if she is more interested in the social aspects of school or her studies. John writes often. He says the church is growing and the ministry is going forward.

Remember that you are always in our thoughts and prayers,
Dad

From reading this letter, which of these things can you tell for certain and which things would be considered speculation?

1. **David has been gone for two weeks:**

   Definite ☐   **Speculation** ☐

2. **David is coming home for Thanksgiving:**

   Definite ☐   **Speculation** ☐

3. **David is a college student:**

   Definite ☐   **Speculation** ☐

4. **David is a Christian:**

   Definite ☐   **Speculation** ☐

5. Mark and David were friends:
    Definite ☐   Speculation ☐

6. Mark and David have known each other for a long time:
    Definite ☐   Speculation ☐

7. David's mother has been sick:
    Definite ☐   Speculation ☐

8. David's mother enjoys getting David's letters:
    Definite ☐   Speculation ☐

9. John and Sheila are brother and sister:
    Definite ☐   Speculation ☐

10. John is a minister:
    Definite ☐   Speculation ☐

Teach me, LORD, the way of your decrees, that I may follow it to the end. Give me understanding, so that I may keep your law and obey it with all my heart.
PSALM 119:33–34

Just as it's difficult to understand fully the content of the letter to David from his father, it is sometimes difficult to understand the intent of Paul's letters to the church. Because we cannot hear both sides of the conversation and because we are trying to understand a culture that we're not familiar with, the intent of the writing is not always clear.

However, the task is not insurmountable. In comparing the apostle's various writings, studying the language and culture of the times, and with the illumination given to us by the Holy Spirit, the task may be challenging but not impossible. Although it's good to remember that we will not always have all the answers, God does choose to reveal Himself to us. Jeremiah 29:13 tells us, *"You will seek me and find me when you seek me with all your heart."*

As you work through these studies, I pray that God will reveal His purposes to your heart.

Write a prayer that God will open your eyes to His intended purposes.

Lord, I pray...

_____

_____

_____

_____

_____

_____

_____

Paul's Letter to the Corinthians

Shortly after leaving Athens, the apostle Paul visited Corinth during his second missionary journey. Unfortunately Corinth, considered one of the greatest commercial centers of the Roman Empire, had a reputation for immorality. Paul founded the church of Corinth amid a backdrop of wickedness.

Read Acts 18:1–3.

Whom did Paul meet in Corinth?

_____

Why did Aquila and Priscilla leave Italy?

_____

_____

In AD 49, the emperor Claudius issued a decree expelling Jews from Rome because of riots in the city over the teachings of Christ. Aquila and Priscilla were among those that had been expelled. It is uncertain how Aquila and Priscilla were converted to Christianity. Some scholars believe they were converted under the preaching of Roman Jews who were present at Jerusalem during the outpouring of the Holy Spirit at Pentecost.[4]

---

4. French L. Arrington and Roger Stronstad, eds., *Full Life Bible Commentary to the New Testament* (Grand Rapids, MI: Zondervan Publishing House, 1999), 630.

Although Aquila had originally come from Pontus in Asia Minor, he evidently became a resident of Rome. However, after Claudius' decree that compelled Jews to leave Rome, Aquila and Priscilla settled in Corinth for a time. When the trouble subsided in Rome, many Jews returned to the city. Aquila and Priscilla eventually returned to Rome after visits to both Corinth and Ephesus.[5]

Why did Paul choose to reside with Aquila and Priscilla?

_____

_____

Read Acts 18:4–18.

Who came from Macedonia to meet Paul?

_____

Why did Paul discontinue his preaching in the synagogue?

_____

_____

After the Jews continued to reject the gospel, Paul demonstratively shook out his clothes in protest. Proclaiming that he was clear from his responsibility to the Jews, Paul proceeded to devote his energies to reaching the Gentiles. At this point Paul also left the Jewish synagogue and began preaching in a location more conducive to ministering to the Gentiles.

Where did Paul go to continue his teaching after leaving the synagogue?

_____

_____

_____

What was the result of this teaching?

_____

_____

_____

Paul's turning away from the Jews to minister to the Gentiles did not mean that he had given up on them. Sometimes we need to step away from a situation in order to let God continue His work; however, in doing so, we continue to pray that God will complete what He began in His way and in His timing.

_____

5. Arrington and Stronstad, *Full Life Bible Commentary*, 630–631.

Corinth, located just south of the ten-mile isthmus that connects central Greece with the Peloponnesus, was considered a strategic trade route. Ephesus and Corinth, both considered important cities and ports, were situated across from each other on the Aegean Sea. Ships, in an effort to avoid a two-hundred-mile trip around Cape Malea, could harbor in Corinth and have their cargoes transported across the isthmus and loaded onto ships waiting on the other side.[6]

Largely due to the Greek culture and language of Corinth, the city was famous for its art, architecture, courts of law, and pagan temples. Unfortunately it also embraced a lifestyle of immorality. The morals of Corinth were so corrupt that "to Corinthianize" came to be associated with living a corrupt and immoral lifestyle.[7]

Theologian Gordon Fee believes that the early church at Corinth consisted predominantly of Gentiles, the majority of them probably in the lower end of the socioeconomic scale. He believes there might also have been two or three wealthy families among the believers. As former pagans, the Corinthians most likely had a Hellenistic (Greek) worldview and attitude concerning ethical behavior. Unfortunately, the immoral culture of Corinth influenced the new Christians.[8]

Problems and divisions arose in the church concerning questionable practices, immorality, factions, lawsuits, abuse of the Lord's Supper, and situations involving the believer's gifts and their ministry in the body of Christ. While Paul was in Ephesus, reports reached him concerning these struggles. In response to these reports, Paul wrote the letter of 1 Corinthians. It is thought to have been written from Ephesus around AD 55, after a second visit by Paul to Corinth. Bible scholars believe that as many as eight or nine letters were written by the apostle Paul to the Corinthian church.[9] Paul himself makes reference to a prior correspondence to 1 Corinthians in 1 Corinthians 5:9. This prior letter is sometimes referred to as the "lost letter."

---

6. Stanley M. Horton, *1 & 2 Corinthians: A Logion Press Commentary* (Springfield, MO: Gospel Publishing, 1999), 9.

7. Ibid., 10.

8. Gordon D. Fee, *The First Epistle to the Corinthians* (Grand Rapids, MI: William B. Eerdmans Publishing Company, 1987), 4.

9. John H. Hayes, ed. *1 Corinthians, 2 Corinthians / William Baird Knox Preaching Guides* (Atlanta: John Knox Press, 1980), 2.

Read 1 Corinthians 1:3–8.

Before endeavoring to correct the problems and clear up any misunderstandings in the church, Paul begins the letter of 1 Corinthians with a greeting and words of encouragement.

What is Paul thankful for concerning the Corinthians?

_____

_____

_____

_____

_____

In *The Full Life Commentary to the New Testament,* Anthony Palma comments on Paul's words of thanksgiving for the Corinthians: "In this thanksgiving section, Paul anticipates matters about which he will soon write...he compliments the believers, even though much of the letter will be corrective in nature. He takes them back to their conversion experience, talks about their present endowment with spiritual gifts, and emphasizes God's enablement in keeping them steadfast until the coming of the Lord."[10]

Do you think it is a good idea to start a discussion involving problems and conflict by complimenting and encouraging the party or parties involved rather than immediately confronting the problem? Why or why not?

_____

_____

_____

_____

_____

_____

And we urge you, brothers and sisters, warn those who are idle and disruptive, encourage the disheartened, help the weak, be patient with everyone.

1 THESSALONIANS 5:14

As was mentioned earlier, problems and divisions arose in the Corinthian church concerning questionable practices, immorality, lawsuits, factions, abuse of the Lord's Supper, and problems involving the believer's

---

10. Arrington and Stronstad, *Full Life Bible Commentary,* 804.

gifts. What types of conflicts or problems might arise in a present day version of the Corinthian church?

_____

_____

_____

_____

_____

_____

Life Scenario

Ephesians is one of four "Prison Epistles" written by Paul during his Roman imprison-ment, AD 61–63. The others include Philippians, Colossians, and Philemon.

A couple with three small children began attending a nearby church. The congregation received them warmly, and the new "family" began attending more regularly and participating in church activities. Shortly afterward, people began to realize that the couple was not married. Some of the members felt that the couple should be approached immediately and confronted about their immoral lifestyle. Others felt that since the couple was making progress spiritually that they should wait and see what might happen. A conflict arose within the church membership as to how the situation should be handled.

How do you think the church should handle this situation?

_____

_____

_____

_____

_____

_____

Paul's Letter to the Ephesians

The book of Ephesians is another epistle where the subject of gifts is men-tioned. However, because there is no direct reference to the Ephesian church in this epistle, and the words "in Ephesus" (Ephesians 1:1) are not found in earlier manuscripts, it is thought to be most likely a circular letter—sent first to the Ephesians and later circulated to other local churches. With this in mind, it's hard to know how much of the information in this epistle directly relates to circumstances surrounding the Ephesian church. But, given the amount of time that Paul spent with these people, it is probably safe to assume the information enclosed in this letter was relevant to their needs and circumstances.

Paul visited Ephesus at the end of his second missionary journey on his homeward trip to Jerusalem. The Ephesian church was established during this time, approximately AD 53. Paul returned to Ephesus a year later during his third missionary journey and stayed for three years.

Ephesus, considered the gateway to Asia because of its strategic location, was considered the entrance for shipping from the West and a point of departure for the caravans traveling between the Ionian coast and the East. Some believe Ephesus was the chief city of Asia Minor in the first century AD.

Ephesus was also a center for magical and occult practices. Paul's teaching about the one true God eventually began to affect the sale of items of magic arts in the city, as well as silver shrines made for the goddess Artemis. Artemis, also known as Diana of the Ephesians, was considered to be the ancient Greek mother goddess and believed to control all fertility. The great Temple of Artemis, one of the Seven Wonders of the Ancient World, was immense in size with carvings and paintings, as well as the image of Artemis, which supposedly fell from heaven.

Read Acts 19:1–12.

What were some of the results of Paul's ministry in Ephesus?

_____

_____

_____

_____

_____

_____

God is not coming to people who merely seek His benefits. He's coming to people who seek His face.
TOMMY TENNEY

Read Acts 19:13–16.

What happened to the Jews who attempted to exorcise demons in the name of Jesus?

_____

_____

_____

_____

_____

_____

Read Acts 19:17–20.

What were the results in Ephesus of this failed attempt to exorcise demons?

_____

_____

_____

_____

_____

_____

Verse 19 tells us that the value of the scrolls (books) burned was fifty thousand drachmas. A drachma was a silver coin worth about a day's wages. Fifty thousand drachmas was a significant amount of money for this time period.

What does Deuteronomy 18:9–14 say about practices of divination and sorcery?

_____

_____

_____

_____

Life Scenario

Jacob is attending a class for "new believers" at Rockford Community Church. During a recent class discussion on the book of Revelation and end-time events, Jacob talked about his involvement in astrology and how it was helpful to him in planning for his future. Jacob wondered what an astrologer might have to say concerning the things predicted in Revelation and concerning end-time events.

How would you respond to Jacob?

_____

_____

_____

_____

Read Acts 19:23–41.

What was the reaction of the silversmiths to Paul's teaching?

_____

_____

_____

_____

_____

_____

...correct, rebuke and encourage—with great patience and careful instruction.

2 TIMOTHY 4:2

From the Temple of Artemis, a street led westward to the city gate, near which there was a stadium built into the side of a mountain. An inscription shows that it was constructed during the reign of Nero, AD 54–68, which would have coincided with the time of Paul's visit to the Ephesian church in AD 53–56. South of this stadium was a theater, also set in the side of the mountain. This theater, believed to have the capacity to accommodate about twenty-five thousand people, was the public auditorium for the city and was thought to be the scene of the riot protesting the apostle Paul's teachings and his supposed attack upon the worship of Artemis.[11]

---

11. Merrill C. Tenney, *New Testament Times* (Grand Rapids, MI: William B. Eerdmans, 1965), 281.

What does the Psalmist say about idols in Psalm 115:1–8?

_____

_____

_____

_____

What "gods" in today's culture do people place before the true God?

_____

_____

_____

_____

What, if anything, are you most tempted to place before the true God?

_____

_____

How can we keep from putting "idols," or "other gods," before the true God?

_____

_____

_____

_____

_____

> *God has planned for us to enjoy the fruit of our labor. But when the enjoyment of this fruit becomes the sole purpose for laboring, idolatry, like a weed, has taken root.*
> **DR. JAMES P. GILLS**

Life Thoughts

The idea of worshipping an idol, like those of Old Testament times, is a concept foreign to our present day society. Worshipping something that we make with our own hands seems foolish to us. But what exactly is an idol? According to the Merriam Webster Student Dictionary, an idol may include something or someone we greatly admire or esteem. Although "admiring" and "esteeming" may not seem like bad things, the idea of putting anything before God is forbidden in the first commandment, "You shall have no other gods before me" (Exodus 20:3). When we put anything before God, we run the risk of worshipping the creation more than the Creator.

Although the results of the uproar in Ephesus indicated there was some protection for Christians that challenged the worship of idols, the local leader's words and actions in quieting the uproar showed he was more concerned with maintaining order in the city than pronouncing a verdict concerning the matter. Although Paul was in some ways vindicated by the authorities, the issue was never completely resolved, and the believers became aware of the monumental task ahead of them in ministering to this cultic community.

Acts 20:1 tells us that after the uproar had ended, Paul sent for the disciples and encouraged them.

Why is it important for Christians to encourage each other during times of trial?

_____

_____

_____

_____

_____

_____

_____

It takes so little to encourage or discourage another person. Will we choose to dampen their spirits or lift them soaring above the obstacles?

Life Scenario

Portia, having experienced a serious car accident and presently undergoing a year of intense physical therapy, is still in a lot of pain and occasionally endures debilitating seizures resulting from her head injury.

While talking to Portia after church one Sunday, one of the associate pastors, Pastor Rick, quoted a Scripture to her telling her that God "will not let you be tempted beyond what you can bear" (1 Corinthians 10:13). Shortly afterward Portia's friend, Cindy, also approached her. After asking how Portia was doing and hearing about all the pain that she was enduring, Cindy hugged her and told her that she was sorry for the all the suffering she was experiencing.

Which approach at comfort do you think Portia might have appreciated most? Why?

_____

_____

_____

_____

_____

_____

_____

Some scholars believe it is impossible to have an objective interpretation of an ancient passage without viewing it in the light of modern perspectives. Although to some extent this may be true, I believe the pursuit is worth the effort.

Paul's Letter to the Romans

The third reference to God's gifts to the believers is mentioned in the book of Romans. Although the apostle Paul had never previously visited Rome, it is generally accepted that he is the author of the book of Romans. Paul wrote this letter to the Christians in Rome sometime around 57 AD after his third missionary journey.

In the first century, Rome was considered one of the most important cities of the Mediterranean world. According to Theologian Joseph A. Fitzmyer, "Rome was originally a shepherd's village, founded as an offshoot of Alba Longa. In time it surpassed its neighboring tribes because of its geographical position in central Italy, near the sea and in command of the ford of the Tiber River."[12] During the time of Paul, Rome may have consisted of a population of approximately eight hundred thousand people, if the suburbs were included. This population, in turn, consisted of many races, including a fair amount of Asian and Jewish influence.[13]

It is uncertain how the Christian community at Rome came to exist. It is generally agreed that it was not founded by any other apostle. Therefore, Paul did not consider Rome the territory of another evangelist. Most likely it developed through the presence of Christians, both Jewish and Gentile, who came to live

---

12.   Joseph A. Fitzmyer, *Romans: A New Translation with Introduction and Commentary.* Vol. 33, in *The Anchor Bible* (New York: Doubleday, 1993), 25.

13.   *The International Standard Bible Encyclopedia,* http://studylight.org/enc/isb/view.cgi?number=T7477 (accessed August 30, 2008).

there under ordinary circumstances, rather than through evangelization of the area. Since Paul neither founded this church nor evangelized this area, he was not intimately acquainted with those to whom he was writing. Therefore, it is likely that the personal references Paul does give to this community have come to him by word of mouth.[14]

Romans 15:19–25 tells us that because Paul recognized that the Roman church was already established, and because he wished to evangelize first those areas where the gospel had not been preached, Paul delayed his visit to the Romans. Later, having completed his work in Asia and Greece, Paul was on his way to Spain with plans to stop and visit the church in Jerusalem to deliver an offering and afterward visit the church in Rome (Romans 15:22–32; Acts 19:21).

Life Scenario

Some of the members of Oakridge Church recently returned from a missions trip to an inner city. As a result of the church's evangelistic outreach during the trip, forty-six people acknowledged Christ as Savior. After the missions team returned from their trip, Pastor Sally encouraged others in the congregation to choose a name from the inner-city "new-converts" list and begin writing to that person, encouraging him or her in their newfound faith. Audrey, who is a member at Oakridge Church, chose a young lady named Megan to correspond with.

What kinds of things could Audrey write to Megan about since the two women have never met? How could Audrey encourage Megan in her newfound beliefs?

_____
_____
_____
_____
_____
_____

Although Paul never reached Rome while on his missionary journeys, he wrote one of his longest letters to the disciples there. He must have cared very deeply for this special group of people whom he had never met.

14. Fitzmyer, *Romans*, 30–33.

Life Thoughts

As I think about this lesson, I remember Carrie, a lady who visited our church years ago, and made a commitment to become a Christian. I befriended her and gave her my phone number in case she should have any questions or need some encouragement. I made a point of greeting her when I saw her in church and asking how she was doing.

Within a few weeks, however, Carrie realized she had an alcohol problem that she could no longer ignore. She called me in tears, explaining how she had become so drunk that she passed out and her young daughter was found wandering the streets unattended. She told me of her decision to enter a one-year Christian drug and alcohol center. She knew that by giving up her job, she could lose her home, but she also knew that by continuing without help she could lose her family and everything that was truly important to her.

Carrie made arrangements to have her children cared for and then entered the program. She was allowed to write letters to friends and family and eventually to make trips home. I wrote letters to her throughout her stay.

At first the letters were difficult for me to write. I had never had an alcohol problem and I found it hard to relate to Carrie's situation. I felt inadequate and wondered how I could possibly say anything in my letters that would help her. Carrie didn't seem to mind, however, and as time went on, I found it easier to write. I shared newsy letters about the church and my family, and anything else I felt might be of interest to her. She seemed to appreciate the letters, and I realized, as time went on, that Carrie didn't need advice concerning her addictions. She had all the help she needed at the center. What Carrie needed was to hear from a friend, and for that I was qualified.

Summary

Although the churches in Ephesus, Rome, and Corinth were different in their cultural situations, all three of these churches shared a common bond—a newfound faith. The apostle Paul recognized the struggles that these new believers would encounter and continued to maintain contact with them through correspondence, as well as by sending ambassadors to encourage and admonish them in their various situations.

In this first lesson, we studied the historical context of the churches in Rome, Corinth, and Ephesus, to which Paul would later write concerning the subject of spiritual gifts. I pray that this brief view into the world of the New Testament will be helpful as we endeavor to understand the churches to which Paul first taught his message concerning God's enabling gifts to believers.

Write a prayer that God will give you understanding into the message given to the early church, as well as its intended message for the church of today.

Lord, I pray…

_____

_____

_____

_____

_____

_____

_____

_____

_____

_____

Lesson Two
Grace Gifts: Natural or Supernatural?

As we learned in Lesson One, in order for us to understand the significance of a Scripture passage, it's important that we understand something about the time period in which it was written as well as the people who lived in that time period. In this lesson, we will explore another key element in understanding Scripture—interpreting the writing itself. This will include a study of the theme or intent of the passage and any related Scripture that might help us to have a better understanding of the context of what was being said. For example, if we randomly pick out a paragraph to read in a book, we might find that there is a crying baby in the story. If we look back to the preceding paragraph, we might also learn that the baby has an upset stomach. This helps us to understand why the baby is crying. Later in the book, the doctor might diagnose the baby with colic. When we take all these bits of information together, we understand more about why the baby is crying. The same is true in Scripture. By reading a Scripture in its context and comparing it with other Scripture we can get a better picture of what is being conveyed by the author.

You have already learned some things about the history and culture of Rome, Corinth, and Ephesus, and you are ready to compare the themes, concepts, and language in the three passages we are studying. By doing this, you will be equipped to understand the truths being communicated and their application and relevance to your life today.

Does this sound impossible? It's easier than you think. With the help of numerous study resources available to the church today, we can search the Scriptures and come to our own conclusions as to their intent. You can do this!

Read Romans 12:1–13; Ephesians 4:1–16; and 1 Corinthians 12:1–31 and write the theme or themes for each of these Scripture passages.

Romans 12:1–13

_____

_____

_____

_____

_____

_____

Ephesians 4:1–16

_____

_____

_____

_____

_____

_____

1 Corinthians 12:1–31

_____

_____

_____

_____

_____

Do you see any common theme or themes in these passages? If so, what are they?

_____

_____

_____

_____

Do you think these themes are applicable for the church today? Why or why not?

_____

_____

_____

_____

_____

_____

_____

_____

Paul's answer to the various circumstances and problems in the churches of Rome, Corinth, Ephesus, and the surrounding communities to which Paul wrote, was unity—unity of the members of the body of Christ practiced in love. Just as this message was critical to the ministry of the New Testament church, so it is important for the church today.

Who could have imagined that when the apostle Paul addressed the letter of 1 Corinthians to *"the church of God in Corinth, to those sanctified in Christ Jesus and called to be his holy people, together with all those everywhere who call on the name of our Lord Jesus Christ—their Lord and ours"* (1 Corinthians 1:2) that he would be reaching such a vast and timeless audience.

Beloved, God cares no more about me than we.
BETH MOORE

Defining Gifts

Although the apostle Paul mentions the concepts of "unity" and "gifts" in all three of these Scripture passages—Romans, 1 Corinthians, and Ephesians—he does not make much of an attempt to give a definition of what he means by "gift" or even to define the individual gifts themselves.

Theologian James F. Stitzinger believes that the most important issue in the understanding of spiritual gifts is their biblical definition and false assumptions that lead to unwarranted conclusions.[1]

What initial definition would you give for the term "gift" as used in these Scripture passages? Since the goal of this study is to define the mean-

---

1. James F. Stitzinger, "Spiritual Gifts: Definitions and Kinds," *Master's Seminary Journal* vol. 14, no. 2 (2003): 149.

ing of "gifts" and their purpose in ministry, your definition may change by the end of this study. However, for now write a general definition of what you think this term might mean.

_____

_____

_____

_____

When considering the meaning of a particular Bible passage, it's helpful to study the early Greek and Hebrew texts. All languages are not the same and there can be difficulties in translating them. It is even more difficult to translate an ancient Scripture passage into today's vernacular. This might be part of the reason for the occasional differences in Bible translations. Since most people reading the Bible are not familiar with these ancient languages, it is helpful to use various study resources such as "lexicons." Lexicons are similar to dictionaries and can help us to compare words from the early Greek and Hebrew manuscripts with words in Scripture passages in the languages of today. Although it is not always advisable to rely on a word-for-word translation in any language, lexicons can be helpful in giving a general idea of individual word meanings.

Greek, considered a world language during the first century, was the language Paul used to write letters to the early church.

Gift

The Greek word for *gift/gifts* in the Romans 12 and 1 Corinthians 12–14 passages is **charisma/charismata**. This Greek word might remind you of an English word that is spelled the same way. However, although our English definition of **charisma** refers to *an ability to inspire or have enthusiasm*, the Greek for **charisma** has a far different meaning, denoting *that which is freely and graciously given as a favor bestowed or an expression of divine grace*. It is often translated simply *gift*.

According to theologian Anthony D. Palma, the word charisma, "gift," occurs in the New Testament a total of seventeen times. All usages are attributable to the writings of the apostle Paul (Romans 1:11; 5:15–16; 6:23; 11:29; 12:6; 1 Corinthians 1:7; 7:7; 12:4, 9, 28, 30, 31; 2 Corinthians 1:11; 1 Timothy 4:14; 2 Timothy 1:6) with one exception (1 Peter 4:10). The word is used in both a broad and restrictive sense, with varying definitions referring to: the whole of redemption (Romans 5:15–16; 6:23); gifts bestowed upon Israel (Romans 11:29); rescue from danger (2 Corinthians 1:11); eternal life (Romans 6:23); and in speaking of special gifts or manifestations used in community for the benefit of the church, such as those references in Romans 12:6 and 1 Corinthians 12:4, 9, 28, 30, 31.[2]

Palma, along with most scholars, believes that in the Romans 12 and 1 Corinthians 12 passages we are studying, the definition of *gifts/charismata* refers to special gifts or manifestations used in community for the benefit of others.

Romans 12:6–8:

> [6] *We have different gifts [**charismata**], according to the grace given to each of us. If your gift is prophesying, then prophesy in accordance with your faith;* [7] *if it is serving, then serve; if it is teaching, then teach;* [8] *if it is to encourage, then give encouragement; if it is giving, then give generously; if it is to lead, do it diligently; if it is to show mercy, do it cheerfully.*

1 Corinthians 12:4–11:

> [4] *There are different kinds of gifts [**charismata**], but the same Spirit distributes them.* [5] *There are different kinds of service, but the same Lord.* [6] *There are different kinds of working, but in all of them and in everyone it is the same God at work.*
>
> [7] *Now to each one the manifestation of the Spirit is given for the common good.* [8] *To one there is given through the Spirit a message of wisdom, to another a message of knowledge by means of the same Spirit,* [9] *to another faith by the same Spirit, to another gifts [**charismata**] of healing by that one Spirit,* [10] *to another miraculous powers, to another prophecy, to another distinguishing between spirits, to another speaking in different kinds of tongues, and to still another the interpretation of tongues.* [11] *All these are the work of one and the same Spirit, and he distributes them to each one, just as he determines.*

In the Ephesians 4 passage we are studying, the Greek word for *gift* is different from the word used in Romans 12 and 1 Corinthians 12. However, although the Greek word for *gift* in Ephesians 4:8 is **doma** (or **domata**, "gifts") rather

---

2. Anthony Palma, "Spiritual Gifts—Basic Considerations," *Pneuma* vol. 1, no 2 (Fall 1979): 4–5.

than **charisma**, it is thought by many Bible scholars that the Ephesians 4 passage should be included with the Romans and Corinthians passage in the apostle Paul's teaching concerning gifts because of the common terminologies and themes of the passages.

Ephesians 4:8–11

*8 This is why it says: "When he ascended on high, he took many captives and gave gifts [**domata**] to his people." 9 (What does "he ascended" mean except that he also descended to the lower, earthly regions? 10 He who descended is the very one who ascended higher than all the heavens, in order to fill the whole universe.) 11 So Christ himself gave the apostles, the prophets, the evangelists, the pastors and teachers.*

How is a gift that you have received different from something you have obtained for yourself?

_____

_____

_____

_____

_____

Who pays for a gift, the giver or receiver?

_____

Grace Gifts

What common word do you see in the following passages concerning spiritual gifts?

Romans 12:3–6

3 For by the _____ given me I say to every one of you: Do not think of yourself more highly than you ought, but rather think of yourself with sober judgment, in accordance with the faith God has distributed to each of you. 4 For just as each of us has one body with many members, and these members do not all have the same function, 5 so

*in Christ we, though many, form one body, and each member belongs
to all the others. ⁶ We have different gifts, according to the _____
given to each of us. If your gift is prophesying, then prophesy in accordance with your faith.*

Ephesians 4:7–8

*⁷ But to each one of us _____ has been given as Christ apportioned
it. ⁸ This is why it says: "When he ascended on high, he took many captives and gave gifts to his people."*

The Greek word for *grace* is **charis**, which may be translated: *grace, kindness,
mercy, goodwill, favor, blessing, gift.* **Charis/grace** is also a form of the word
gift/charisma.

What significance, if any, do you think the word grace/charis has to the word gift/charisma?

_____
_____
_____
_____
_____
_____

*Grace is getting
what we don't
deserve. Mercy is
not getting what
we do deserve.*
AUTHOR UNKNOWN

Some Christians refer to **charismata** as "grace-gifts." These gifts may be
thought of as God's expression of divine grace.

According to theologian Joseph Fitzmyer, each member must realize the social
character of the God-given talents and make use of them for the common good
without envy or jealously of gifts given to other members. Gifts have been given
so that with them Christians might serve one another. All **gifts/charismata**
are graces that move Christians to action on behalf of others.³

---

3. Fitzmyer, *Romans*, 646–647.

Life Thoughts

As I am writing this, I am sitting on the patio of my brother-in-law and his wife's home, stopping periodically to gather my thoughts and to let their dogs Gracie, a miniature dachshund, and Selah, a miniature pinscher, in and out the patio door. As I watch their contented interaction on this particular day, I think back to moments when their times together are not quite so peaceful. I continue to be amazed how one minute Gracie can be a sweet and lovable companion to Selah and the next minute growling and baring her teeth should Selah come anywhere near her food. I am even more amazed that Selah takes it all in stride, graciously ignoring Gracie's very ungracious ways.

As I sit and watch my companions' present docile and amiable interaction, I think about how often I, like Gracie, refuse to share that which is so freely and graciously given to me, and I ponder how ironic it is that Gracie should have the name that she does.

What examples from the Bible can you think of where grace was bestowed upon believers?

_____
_____
_____
_____
_____
_____

Life Scenario

Tom and Beth were excited. All five of their children were coming home for Christmas. Each of the children brought gifts, and although Tom and Beth knew that the real gift was having their entire family home, they enjoyed opening the various presents their children had selected for them. Each child was different and their gifts reflected their different personalities.

Jessica gave her parents new tennis racquets. Jessica loved sports, and although Tom and Beth were not really involved in sports, they recognized that Jessica had given them a gift that reflected something she loved.

Stephen gave his mother and father a gift certificate for their favorite store. Stephen knew that his parents could use some new things and that money had been tight for them recently.

James gave his father a new designer suit and his mother a diamond bracelet. James was doing well with his new business and he wanted to get something for his parents they would not normally buy for themselves.

Jennifer didn't have a lot of money. She offered to clean her parents' house for them. She knew that her father had been extra busy at work recently and that her mother had not been feeling well.

Brad gave his Mom and Dad a gift basket that he had received from one of his clients at work. Brad had been busy with school and work lately and didn't have a lot of time to shop for Christmas gifts.

Consider the Christmas gifts brought by Tom and Beth's children:

Do you feel that one gift was more appropriate or better than the others? Why or why not?

_____

_____

_____

_____

_____

_____

_____

_____

_____

_____

What things should you consider when giving a gift?

_____

_____

_____

_____

_____

_____

What things do you think God considers when giving us gifts?

_____

_____

_____

_____

_____

_____

Peter also briefly mentions the subject of *gifts/charismata* in 1 Peter 4:10–11.

Read 1 Peter 4:10–11. What does Peter say concerning gifts/charismata in this passage?

_____

_____

_____

_____

_____

_____

As was mentioned earlier, all languages are not the same and there can be difficulty in translating any of them. Sometimes a word in one language might not be easy to translate into another. Translating an ancient language into today's vernacular can be even more complicated. This is the case with the Greek word *charismata*, which we translate into our English language as *gifts*. Unfortunately, there is no one word in our English language to translate adequately the full meaning of this ancient Greek word. In our English vernacular, we tend to think of *gifts* as things given to us for our own personal use; however, the Greek translation of *gifts/charismata* encompasses more than what our English word for *gifts* implies. God's *gifts/charismata* are not given to us for our own benefit, but rather are expressions of divine *grace/charis* that work through us in conjunction with other gifted members of the body of Christ. These gifts should be used in service to God and to bring glory to Him.

Think back to the scenario about the gifts that Tom and Beth's children gave to them for Christmas. How are these gifts different from the gifts/ charismata God gives to us as Christians?

_____

_____

_____

_____

_____

_____

_____

_____

_____

_____

Natural or Supernatural Gifts?

Christians continue to debate whether or not gifts should be viewed as natural, supernatural, a combination of both, or whether they should simply be considered as God-given enablements without any distinction as to their natural or supernatural capabilities. Theologians, Bible scholars, pastors, teachers, and church members are divided on this subject.

Paul's Gift Lists

Make a list of the gifts Paul mentions in the New Testament under the appropriate Scripture passage:

Circle or highlight gifts that are mentioned in more than one passage.

Romans 12:6–8	1 Corinthians 12:8–10 & 12:28	Ephesians 4:11
1. _____	1. _____	1. _____
2. _____	2. _____	2. _____
3. _____	3. _____	3. _____
4. _____	4. _____	4. _____
5. _____	5. _____	5. _____
6. _____	6. _____	
7. _____	7. _____	
	8. _____	
	9. _____	
	10. _____	
	11. _____	
	12. _____	
	13. _____	

Christian leaders throughout the church are becoming more open to the possibility that the apostle Paul might have intended both natural and supernatural gifts in his gift lists, and that there might be less of a distinction between the two than was originally thought. David Lim, theologian and pastor, believes there are two views regarding the natural and supernatural make-up of gifts. "The first view equates the gifts with natural talents dedicated to the Lord... A second view characterizes the gifts as totally supernatural, denying human faculties... Because some have thought of the gifts as totally supernatural, they have emphasized the more spectacular gifts to the detriment of the less spectacular gifts."[4] Lim believes that it is not biblical to accept either of these extreme positions.

Others continue to believe that the gifts in Paul's lists should only be considered supernatural. They believe that these gifts are given after conversion and should in no way be associated with natural abilities which rely on natural power rather than the endowment of the Spirit.

Do you think the apostle Paul's gift lists include only supernatural gifts or a combination of both supernatural and natural gifts—or that he did not intend any distinction at all? Why do you believe as you do?

_____

_____

_____

_____

_____

_____

_____

There are many of us willing to do great things for the Lord, but few of us are willing to do little things.

D. L. MOODY

Another disagreement among Christians involves the terminology of the phrase *spiritual gifts*. Although the gifts in Paul's gift lists are often referred to as *spiritual gifts*, Bible scholars and theologians are divided on the definition of what is meant by the word *spiritual*, or whether or not the gifts should even be labeled as such.

Some Christians believe Paul's gift list in 1 Corinthians 12 contains gifts that are more *spiritual* than the ones mentioned in Paul's other lists in Romans and Ephesians because the word *gifts* is added to the word *spiritual* in some translations, thereby transforming the word **spiritual/pneumatikos** into the phrase *spiritual gifts*. Other Christians disagree because the words **spiritual/pneumatikos** and **gifts/charismata** are not actually used together in the Greek manuscripts of this verse, but rather the word **spiritual/pneumatikos** is used alone. According to these Christians, Paul might have been simply

---

4. David Lim, *Spiritual Gifts: A Fresh Look* (Springfield, MO: Gospel Publishing House, 1991), 43–44.

introducing his subject of discourse by referring to "spiritual things," or "matters of the Spirit," rather than referring exclusively to "gifts." In other words, he may have been referring to spiritual matters in general and not solely to gifts.

Because of these differences in translations, some Christians believe too much emphasis is placed on the word *spiritual* in regards to *gifts*, and that it is not always defined in the way it should be. These Christians believe the word *spiritual* is often falsely equated with the word *miraculous*. David Lim believes it is crucial to the understanding of gifts to realize that the opposite of *spiritual* is not *physical*, but *sinful, carnal*. Christians must remember that they are redeemed and that God seeks to perfect the image of Christ in them. He emphasizes that *physical* should not be equated with *carnal*, just as *spiritual* is not equated with *spectacular*.[5]

What do you think?

Do you think the word *spiritual* means *miraculous*? Why or why not?

_____

_____

_____

_____

_____

_____

Life Scenario

Eric loves playing the piano. Music has always come easy for him. Eric's parents, realizing his love for music, hired a piano teacher for Eric when he was only six years old. Eric eventually learned to read music as well as play "by ear."

When Eric's church asked him to join their worship team, Eric was excited. He would now be able to combine the music that he loved with Christian ministry. Eric's parents were proud of him. They loved to hear him play the piano during worship services. They recognized their son was blessed with a very special ministry.

---

5.   Lim, *Spiritual Gifts: A Fresh Look*, 44.

As Eric was playing the piano one Sunday during a worship service, Eric's mother noticed a difference in his playing. Having listened to Eric play the piano many times, she was well aware of his capabilities. Today, however, she was noticing something different. Eric was playing music beyond even his own abilities. The guitar player stopped playing and watched as Eric continued to play the piano during the service. She too was sensing there was something different about Eric's playing.

Would you say that Eric's playing can be distinguished as either natural or supernatural? Why or why not?

_____

_____

_____

_____

If you are still uncertain as to Paul's intent concerning natural and/or supernatural gifts, or whether there should be any distinction at all in God's gifts to his people, you may have a better idea after we attempt to define the various gifts in the apostle's gift lists. If not, that is okay. As you can see, not even the "experts" agree. It is more important that we understand God has an individual plan for each of our lives and He has equipped us with the means to fulfill that plan according to His kingdom purpose.

Read Psalm 139:13–16 and Jeremiah 1:5.

What do these verses tell us about God's unique plan for our lives?

_____

_____

_____

_____

_____

"For I know the plans I have for you," declares the LORD, "plans to prosper you and not to harm you, plans to give you hope and a future."
JEREMIAH 29:11

Life Thoughts

God has uniquely formed us and nothing He does is by chance or accident. As we study Paul's gift lists in the weeks ahead, try to imagine the early church and how these special enablements/ministries might have been used to fulfill God's purposes. Think of the gifts also in light of the church today. Think about how God might wish to use these gifts in your own personal life or in the lives of others. Keep in mind that, as in the time of the apostles, the purpose of the gifts is for the ministry of the church in unity, and not to be used independently or for personal benefit. You will never be expected to function as a "lone ranger" Christian, but will always have the support and love of your fellow believers as you journey together in developing the ministries that God has given you.

Pray that in the days ahead, God will open your eyes to the unique way in which you have been created.

Lord I pray...

_____

_____

_____

_____

_____

_____

_____

_____

Lesson Three
The Romans Gift List

Content of Paul's Letter to the Romans

You may recall from Lesson One that we are not certain how the Christian community at Rome came to exist. Since Paul had not previously visited Rome, and he was not intimately acquainted with the Roman believers, he might have thought it necessary to start his letter with more general doctrine before getting into practical teaching. Thus he begins his letter by plainly describing the foundation for the believer's faith: (1) all have sinned, (2) Christ died to provide forgiveness for sins, and (3) through faith we are made right with God. After setting this framework, Paul gives guidelines for the Christian life and its effect on the day-to-day life of the Romans.

In chapters 12–14, Paul gives some practical guidelines about public worship. Paul admonishes the church to present themselves in a way that is pleasing to God rather than conforming to the standards of the world. He further encourages the believers to work together in love, using the gifts God has given individual members in a way that brings unity to the Church and its purpose.

Paul continues his letter by giving advice to the Romans regarding their treatment of others within the church, as well as those outside the church, by instructing them to love their neighbors as themselves. He further instructs the believers at Rome to be mindful of the state of others by being careful not to be judgmental in their relationships or to act in any way that might cause others to stumble.

In this lesson, which outlines Romans 12:1–13, we will focus on Paul's practical guidelines concerning gifts and the body of Christ. Paul introduces this teaching by admonishing the believers in their personal relationship to God, encouraging them not to conform to the standards that are acceptable to the world, but rather offering themselves *continually* as living sacrifices that are acceptable to God. In Romans 12:3–5, Paul further instructs the believers to have humble assessments of their God-given gifts, so their gifts might be understood in the context of the abilities of others, and that the believers might work together as individual parts of a whole.

> *God, whom I serve in my spirit in preaching the gospel of his Son, is my witness how constantly I remember you in my prayers at all times; and I pray that now at last by God's will the way may be opened for me to come to you.*
> **ROMANS 1:9–10**

> *Some think the book of Romans is Paul's most comprehensive epistle in regards to the general understanding of the gospel.*

Read Romans 12:1–8

How are the gifts that Paul lists in this Scripture passage to be used?

_____

_____

_____

_____

He has shown you, O mortal, what is good. And what does the LORD require of you? To act justly and to love mercy and to walk humbly with your God.

MICAH 6:8

Romans 12:6–8 Gift List

What seven gifts does Paul mention in this gift list?

_____

_____

_____

In Romans 12:6–8, Paul emphasizes that God has given individuals different enabling strengths. However, before giving a short list of examples of some of these strengths (gifts), Paul encourages the believers to use their God-given gifts well—in humility and with a willing spirit.

How is it possible to maintain the attitudes of humility and confidence while using the gifts God has given to us?

_____

_____

_____

_____

_____

_____

Humility is the discipline of decreasing the scale of my own story until it fits inside the Jesus story.

EARL CREP

In Romans 12:9–11, following his gift list, Paul gives a short message pointing out that love must be sincere and devoted to be considered true. This love for one another calls on believers to practice hospitality while zealously considering the needs of others, and in this way, honoring each other above themselves.

Gift of Prophecy

The first gift Paul mentions in his Romans gift list is **prophecy**. This gift is listed in all three of Paul's gift lists: Romans 12:6; 1 Corinthians 12:10, 28; and Ephesians 4:11.

The Greek word for **prophecy** used in Romans 12:6 is *propheteia*. As was mentioned earlier, when considering the meaning of a particular Bible passage, it's often helpful to study the language in which the text was originally written. For New Testament passages, this language would be the Koine Greek. We will be using definitions from lexicons, which are similar to dictionaries, to help us compare words from early Greek manuscripts with words in Scripture passages in the languages of today.

> The Greek lexicon definition for *propheteia* used in Romans 12:6 is *prophecy—interpreting divine will or purpose.*

Following are some ideas concerning the **gift of prophecy** and its relationship with our God-given gifts, and how it is viewed by various Bible scholars, theologians, pastors, and teachers. Keep in mind as you read the ***Thoughts from the Experts*** sections throughout this book that these are only some of the varied thoughts concerning the individual giftings and may not encompass the scholar or teacher's full gift definition. Remember also that not all Christians agree in their perspectives concerning the believer's God-given gifts.

THOUGHTS FROM THE EXPERTS ABOUT: THE GIFT OF PROPHECY

- Includes anyone speaking with divine authority whether in the past, present, or the future.[1]

- Provides divine direction and strategies for Christ's body in the world, revealing God's purposes so God's people can influence their generation in the wisest way. The gift of prophecy probably refers to recognized prophets rather than to anyone who occasionally prophesies.[2]

---

1. "Jamieson, Faussett Commentary," http://eword.gospelcom.net/comments/romans/jfb/romans12.htm.
2. Keener, *Gift Giver*, 131.

- Spontaneous, Spirit-inspired, intelligible messages, orally delivered in the gathered assembly, intended for the edification or encouragement of the people.[3]

- Prophecy involves speaking God's instructions by divine inspiration to a person or persons, or for a certain situation.[4]

- "Prophecy, generally speaking, is utterance inspired by the Spirit of God. Biblical prophecy may be by revelation, wherein the prophet proclaims a message previously received through a dream, a vision, or the Word of the Lord."[5]

Read 2 Chronicles 34:21–28

During King Josiah's reforms of the temple, he recovered the Book of the Law and inquired of the Lord through Huldah the prophet concerning the contents of the book. How did Huldah the prophet help Josiah in this instance?

Prophecy is an illusive term that is both reverenced and at times ridiculed.

_____

_____

_____

_____

_____

Read Joel 2:12–13.

How would you describe the prophet Joel's message to Judah?

_____

_____

_____

_____

3. Fee, *The First Epistle to the Corinthians,* 595.

4. Siegfried Grossmann, *There Are Other Gifts than Tongues,* trans. by Susan Wiesmann (Wheaton: Tyndale House Publishers, 1971), 19.

5. Myer Pearlman, *Knowing the Doctrines of the Bible* (Springfield, MO: Gospel Publishing House, 1937), 324.

Read 1 Corinthians 14:3.

What does Paul say about prophecy in this Scripture?

_____

_____

_____

Life Scenario

A man, speaking at a small town church, seemed to have miraculous knowledge about the lives of the individuals in the church. He even predicted future events concerning the church and some of its members. His messages were uplifting and positive.

But the church was mixed in its feelings about the man. Some in the congregation were excited about the prospect of the future events foretold by the man, but others were skeptical. After a year's time, very few of the man's predictions had come to pass.

Do you think this man had the gift of prophecy? Why or why not?

_____

_____

_____

_____

_____

_____

Write your own definition for the *gift of prophecy*.

_____

_____

_____

_____

_____

_____

Dear friends, do not believe every spirit, but test the spirits to see whether they are from God, because many false prophets have gone out into the world.

1 JOHN 4:1

Gift of Service

The next gift in Paul's list of gifts in Romans is **service** (some translations say **ministry**).

The Greek word for service in Romans 12:7 is *diakonia*.

> The Greek lexicon definition for *diakonia* used in Romans 12:7 is *service* or *ministry*.

THOUGHTS FROM THE EXPERTS ABOUT: THE GIFT OF SERVICE

The race to be a leader is crowded, but the field is wide open for those willing to be servants.
RICK WARREN

- Care for any kind of practical need that might surface in the membership.[6]

- "...the capacity to provide assistance in meeting practical needs, thus making life a little easier for others. Often this gift concerns sacrificial, behind-the-scenes assistance and benefits others by freeing them up for vital ministries."[7]

- "The gift of service is the special ability that God gives to certain members of the Body of Christ to identify the unmet needs involved in a task related to God's work, and to make use of available resources to meet those needs and help accomplish the desired goals."[8]

- The gift of service involves doing what is necessary in a right way. It is the gift of selflessness because it involves working for others rather than self.[9]

---

6. Robert H. Mounce, ed., *The New American Commentary: An Exegetical and Theological Exposition of Holy Scripture, Romans* vol. 27 (USA: Broadman & Holman Publishers, 1995), 235.

7. Aubrey Malphurs. *Maximizing Your Effectiveness: How to Discover and Develop Your Divine Design.* 2nd ed. (Grand Rapids, MI: Baker Books, 2006), 50.

8. C. Peter Wagner, *Your Spiritual Gifts Can Help Your Church Grow* (Glendale, CA: GL Regal Books Division/GL Publications, 1980), 259.

9. Grossmann, *There Are Other Gifts than Tongues*, 36, 40.

Read Acts 6:1–4.

How is the example of service or "waiting on tables" used in this Bible passage?

_____

_____

_____

What examples of the gift of service do you see evident in today's church?

_____

_____

_____

_____

_____

Write your own definition for the *gift of service*.

_____

_____

_____

_____

_____

Gift of Teaching

Paul's third gift in his Roman's discourse is **teaching**. Like prophecy, **teaching** is also listed in all three of Paul's gift lists.

The Greek word for **teaching** in Romans 12:7 is ***didaskalia***.

> The Greek lexicon definition for ***didaskalia*** used in Romans 12:7 is *the act of teaching, instruction.*

If you give me a fish, I'll eat for today. If you teach me how to fish, I'll eat for a lifetime.
CHINESE PROVERB

THOUGHTS FROM THE EXPERTS ABOUT: THE GIFT OF TEACHING

- An ancient and honorable profession in the Jewish culture. In the New Testament world, teaching was primarily but not exclusively moral instruction.[10]

- The gift of teaching is the God-given ability to understand and communicate biblical truth. It is not simply the ability to teach any truth.[11]

- "Those with the gift of teaching are focused on the questions and concerns of their audience, and manage to impart their knowledge in an interesting and stimulating manner."[12]

- "The God-given special ability to serve and strengthen the body of Christ by teaching sound doctrine in relevant ways, empowering people to gain a sound and mature spiritual education."[13]

Read Acts 18:24-26.

Whom did Priscilla and Aquila meet while in Ephesus?

_____

How did they help this new convert?

_____

_____

_____

_____

_____

Read James 3:1.

What does James say about teachers in this Scripture passage?

_____

_____

What is taught a student outside the class room is just as important as that which is taught within the classroom, for it is taught by example.

---

10. Mounce, *The New American Commentary*, 235.

11. Malphurs, *Maximizing Your Effectiveness*, 52.

12. Christian A. Schwarz, *The 3 Colors of Ministry* (St. Charles, IL: ChurchSmart Resources, 2001), 123.

13. Erik Rees, *S.H.A.P.E.* (Grand Rapids, MI: Zondervan, 2006), 44.

Read 1 Timothy 1:3–7.

What does Paul tell Timothy about some that desire to be teachers?

_____

_____

_____

_____

_____

Write your own definition for the *gift of teaching*.

_____

_____

_____

_____

I long to see you so that I may impart to you some spiritual gift to make you strong—that is, that you and I may be mutually encouraged by each other's faith.
ROMANS 1:11–12

Life Thoughts

While walking to the store one day, I followed behind a mother and her two small boys. As we continued to walk, I was surprised to see the mother stop and stomp on a beer can until it was flat against the sidewalk. She did not pick the flattened can up, nor did she make any comment when she had finished.

I am not sure why she crushed the can. Perhaps she does not like beer, or perhaps she just enjoys crushing cans. I wondered what she was teaching her children by her action.

Gift of Encouragement

Have you ever had someone encourage you? What did that mean to you? The apostle Paul's next gift in his gift list is **encouragement**. This might seem like an unlikely gift to be considered important enough to be in Paul's gift list. However, if you have ever been on the receiving end of a word of encouragement, you know how special this gift can be.

The Greek word for **encouragement (exhortation)** in Romans 12:8 is *paraklesis*.

> The Greek lexicon definition for *paraklesis* used in Romans 12:8 is *(1) The act of emboldening another in belief or course of action, encouragement, exhortation. (2) lifting of another's spirits, comfort, consolation.*

THOUGHTS FROM THE EXPERTS ABOUT: THE GIFT OF ENCOURAGEMENT

- "The God-given special ability to serve and strengthen the body of Christ by helping others to live God-centered lives through inspiration, encouragement, counseling, and empowerment."[14]

- "The gift of encouragement (or exhortation) involves encouraging, consoling, and, when necessary, confronting and admonishing others so they are benefited spiritually in their walk with Christ. Christians with this gift have an unusual sensitivity to, and are attracted to, those who are discouraged or struggling."[15]

- "The gift of exhortation involves the supernatural ability to come alongside to help, to strengthen the weak, reassure the wavering, buttress the buffeted, steady the faltering, console the troubled, encourage the halting."[16]

Read Acts 4:36.

What does Barnabas's name mean?

_____

Read Acts 9:26–27.

How might Barnabas have been an encouragement to Saul/Paul?

_____

_____

_____

---

14. Rees, *S.H.A.P.E.*, 39.
15. Malphurs, *Maximizing Your Effectiveness*, 49.
16. Leslie B. Flynn, *19 Gifts of the Spirit*, (Wheaton: Victor Books, A division of SP Publications, 1975), 82.

Read Acts 11:22–23.

In what way did Barnabas encourage the Christians at Antioch?

_____

_____

Life Thoughts

Marcia, one of my closest friends, is someone I greatly admire. Over the years, while raising six children, Marcia not only found time for her own personal prayer and Bible study, but managed to fit in a devotional time with her children before school as well.

Marcia was an example to me, not only as a Christian friend, but also as an example of a Christian mother. As our children grew, I always listened closely to any child-rearing advice that Marcia might have. Her children were a few years older than mine, so I considered her advice as a warning for what was ahead. She always seemed to handle everything so well.

Our children are grown now, but as mothers we still pray for them and sometimes call each other when we need extra prayer support. As we talked on the phone this particular day, we shared some of our parenting woes. Parenting had been more difficult than we had thought and we had certainly made a lot of mistakes. Marcia told me that I had been a good mother to my children, that I had done a good job, and that I had done my best. And then she paused before continuing. What she said next surprised me: "I wish someone had told me that."

I was stunned by Marcia's words. To me, she had always been the example of a wonderful Christian mother. Through all these years, how did I miss the opportunity to tell her how I felt?

To the world you may be one person, but to one person you may be the world.
UNKNOWN

Who can you encourage this week? Maybe, like Marcia, someone simply needs to be told that they are doing a good job. List some people you can encourage.

_____

_____

_____

Write your own definition for the *gift of encouragement*.

_____

_____

_____

Gift of Giving

The next word in Paul's gift list is **giving**—some translations say **contributing to the needs of others**. The Greek word for **giving** in Romans 12:8 is *metadidomi*.

> The Greek lexicon definition for *metadidomi* used in Romans 12:8 is *give, impart, share*.

THOUGHTS FROM THE EXPERTS ABOUT: THE GIFT OF GIVING

- Individuals who give a significant percentage beyond their tithe to the kingdom of God.[17]

- "The gift of giving is the ability to give eagerly, wisely, generously, and sacrificially to others. Regardless of the amount, people with this gift genuinely view their treasures, talents, and time as on loan from God and not their own."[18]

- "The God-given special ability to serve and strengthen the body of Christ by joyfully supporting and funding various kingdom initiatives through material contributions beyond the tithe."[19]

- If a person's gift is contributing to the needs of others, then they should give generously. It is not to be done reluctantly or under compulsion, but cheerfully.[20]

17. Schwarz, *The 3 Colors of Ministry*, 105.
18. Malphurs, *Maximizing Your Effectiveness*, 50.
19. Rees, *S.H.A.P.E*, 40.
20. Mounce, *The New American Commentary*, 235.

Read Romans 12:8.

According to Paul, in what manner should Christians give?

_____

_____

Read Acts 9:36–42.

Do you think Tabitha (Dorcas) illustrated the gift of giving? If so, why?

_____

_____

_____

_____

Read Philippians 4:15–18.

How does Paul describe the gifts given by the Philippian church?

_____

_____

The widow's mite, when blessed by God, is of great value.

Read Luke 21:1–4.

How does Jesus's definition of giving differ from that of the world?

_____

_____

_____

_____

Write your own definition for the *gift of giving*.

_____

_____

_____

_____

Life Scenario

Barry loves to give. He is single and doesn't need a lot of things for himself. He especially loves to give to needy people at Christmas time; however, by January, Barry often does not have enough money to pay his bills or to buy groceries.

Would you give Barry any advice? If so, what would you say?

_____

_____

_____

_____

_____

_____

The Gift of Leadership

The concept of leadership is a popular topic for seminars and forums both inside and outside the church. But what exactly is leadership? Is everyone expected to be a leader or are some people more inclined to be leaders than others?

The Greek word for **the one leading** as mentioned in Romans 12:8 is ***proistamenos***.

> The Greek lexicon definition for ***proistamenos*** used in Romans 12:8 is *to exercise a position of leadership, rule, direct, be at the head of.*

Used with the article in the Greek language, ***proistamenos*** literally means "the one standing in front."

- "The God-given special ability to serve and strengthen the body of Christ by casting vision, stimulating spiritual growth, applying strategies, and achieving success where God's purposes are concerned."[21]

---

21. Rees, *S.H.A.P.E*, 42.

- To set before or set over. It is also related to the function of guardianship or responsibility for those placed under one's jurisdiction.[22]

- "Spirit directed leadership chooses the right action from among various possibilities and moves the whole group in this direction."[23]

Leaders in History

Adolf Hitler, chancellor of Germany from 1933 to 1945, was considered a dictator whose policies precipitated World War II and the Holocaust. One of the foundations of Hitler's social policies was the concept of racial hygiene. Applied to human beings, "survival of the fittest" was interpreted as requiring racial purity and killing off those thought to be unworthy of life.

Benito Mussolini, Italy's fortieth Prime Minister (from 1922 until 1943), is know for creating a fascist state by manipulating the people of Italy with his remarkable charisma. He was said to have had complete control of the media and his political rivals. By leading terror campaigns and using propaganda, he totally did away with the democratic government system that had existed before his leadership.

Mahatma Gandhi, after studying law, became a leader in the Indian freedom struggle against the colonial rule. He eventually led his country to freedom in 1947. He was known for his policy of non-violence and his motivational approach of leading by example.

Dr. Martin Luther King Jr. was best known as a humanitarian and civil rights activist. He led the civil rights movement in the United States from the mid-1950s until his death by assassination in 1968. In 1964, he received the Nobel Peace Prize for combatting racial inequality. King was well known for leading the historic march on Washington, DC, where he delivered his famous speech, "I Have a Dream."

Corrie Ten Boom, the first licensed woman watchmaker in the Netherlands and author of the book *The Hiding Place*, was known for hiding Jews during the World War II Holocaust. After spending time in a German concentration camp for her involvement in these activities, Corrie was released due to a clerical er-

Nearly all men can stand adversity, but if you want to test a man's character, give him power.
ABRAHAM LINCOLN

---

22. Arrington and Stronstad, *Full Life Bible Commentary*, 770.
23. Grossmann, *There Are Other Gifts than Tongues*, 77.

WHAT ARE SPIRITUAL GIFTS?

ror. Subsequently she traveled the world helping other Holocaust victims and sharing a message of God's love and forgiveness.

What are some similarities and differences between a dictator, a leader, and a biblical leader?

_____

_____

_____

_____

_____

_____

_____

_____

As leaders we must always maintain the attitude that people work with us, not for us.

List the characteristics of leadership in each of the following Scripture passages:

2 Chronicles 32:2–8 (Hezekiah)

_____

_____

_____

_____

1 Timothy 3:1–7

_____

_____

_____

_____

_____

Life Scenario

Pastor Tom, pastor of Pointview Tabernacle, was becoming increasingly concerned about the maintenance needed for the fifty-year-old building. He was thankful that the congregation was blessed with Joe, a retired maintenance man who frequently helped the church with its various repair projects. Last week, after a leaky pipe caused some damage to the ceiling, Joe put together a team of volunteers to clean up the mess caused by the leak. He organized them to do what was needed to fix the pipes, repair the ceiling tiles, and to clean up the area when the work was finished. Pastor Tom, who was not known for his maintenance skills, was always glad to give projects of this kind over into the capable hands of Joe, allowing him to take charge of the various maintenance situations when needed.

Who would you say was the leader in this situation? Why?

_____

_____

_____

_____

Write your own definition for the *gift of leadership*.

_____

_____

_____

_____

In the matter of giftings, a leader must learn to relinquish his or her leadership to the one who one is more qualified to facilitate the task at hand.

Life Thoughts

Teaching Vacation Bible School is not always easy—molding a child's actions without squelching their giftedness can be a difficult task, and this particular year proved to be no exception. The Vacation Bible School for the year was based on a concept that used "stations." This meant that my group would be moving to different areas of the church throughout our allotted time together. Knowing that children often like to be first, I designed a system in which the children would take turns being the line leader as we traveled to our different destinations. Sup-

posedly, after each child would take his or her turn leading, they would go to the end of the line and eventually work their way up again as the week progressed.

Most of the children took their turn without a problem; Eddie, however, was an exception. Somehow, no matter who was "supposed" to be first, Eddie would continue to move up to the front of the line until he was leading again. Each time I caught him and sent him back to the end of the line, he would immediately start his forward progress again. Periodically, when Eddie became especially frustrated, he would race off ahead of the group in the direction he thought we were going. Unfortunately, he was often headed in the wrong direction. (I was thankful to have an assistant that year.)

I wouldn't be surprised if one day Eddie becomes a great leader. I can only hope that he figures out where he is going first.

The Gift of Mercy

The Greek word for **mercy** in Romans 12:8 is *eleos*.

> The Greek lexicon definition for *eleos* used in Romans 12:8 is *to be greatly concerned for someone in need, to have compassion, mercy, pity.*

THOUGHTS FROM THE EXPERTS ABOUT: THE GIFT OF MERCY

- "The God-given special ability to serve and strengthen the body of Christ by ministering to those who suffer physically, emotionally, spiritually, or relationally. Their actions are characterized by love, care, compassion, and kindness toward others."[24]

- The ability to put empathy into concrete action. A person who is merciful extends himself or herself to those in need.[25]

- "The gift of showing mercy is the Spirit-guided ability to manifest practical, compassionate, cheerful love toward suffering members of the body of Christ."[26]

---

24. Rees, *S.H.A.P.E*, 43.
25. Arrington and Stronstad, *Full Life Bible Commentary*, 771.
26. Flynn, *19 Gifts of the Spirit*, 133.

Because of the LORD's great love we are not consumed, for his compassions never fail. They are new every morning; great is your faithfulness.
LAMENTATIONS 3:22–23

Read Romans 12:8.

How should the gift of mercy be used?

_____

In what kind of activities might a person with the gift of mercy be involved?

_____

_____

_____

Read Luke 10:29–37.

What reason was given for the Good Samaritan stopping to care for the man who had fallen into the hands of robbers?

_____

_____

Read Ephesians 2:4–6.

What does this Scripture tell us about God's mercy?

_____

_____

_____

_____

What problems might a person who has the gift of mercy encounter?

_____

_____

_____

_____

Blessed are the merciful, for they will be shown mercy.
MATTHEW 5:7

Like many of the gifts, mercy is a characteristic that all Christians should possess. However, there are those who seem to be extra gifted in showing mercy to others.

55

Write your own definition for the *gift of mercy*.

_____
_____
_____
_____

Write a prayer asking God to show you any of the gifts in the Roman's list that may be evident in either your family members or in you. Ask Him to reveal His purposes concerning these gifts in your lives.

Lord I pray...

_____
_____
_____
_____
_____
_____
_____
_____
_____
_____

Lesson Four
The 1 Corinthians 12:8–10 Gift List

The Corinthians and Gifts

You might remember from Lesson One that the church at Corinth was born amidst a city plagued with immorality and cultic practices. Although the new Christians desired to turn from these sinful practices and follow the teachings that Paul and his companions had presented to them, they struggled at times with how this was to be accomplished. Some of these questions involved the usage of gifts in the church.

According to theologian Gordon Fee, it's most likely that the 1 Corinthians 12 teachings on gifts and the body of Christ were in answer to questions raised in correspondence from the Corinthian church; however, it is difficult to determine what the Corinthians might have said in their letter to elicit such a response from Paul. Fee believes that Paul's answer was intended to be both instructive and corrective.[1]

In chapters 12–14, Paul gives the church at Corinth a more complete teaching and understanding of gifts and their relationship to the body of Christ, as well as instruction concerning misuse of the gifts. By encouraging the church to recognize the value of the gifts as well as the individuals that possess them, Paul further instructs the believers to work together by avoiding favoritism or petty quarrels that might result in divisions.

1 Corinthians 12:8–10 Gift List

In this letter to the Corinthians, Paul reintroduces the subject of gifts by telling the believers he does not wish them to be ignorant concerning spiritual things. Throughout his instructional and corrective teaching in chapter 12, Paul gives various examples of gifts.

---

1. Fee, *The First Epistle to the Corinthians*, 570.

What nine gifts does Paul mention in 1 Corinthians 12:8–10?

_____

_____

_____

_____

Paul lists nine gifts in 1 Corinthians 12:8–10. Because we have already discussed the gift of prophecy, which was included in the Romans list, we will concentrate on the remaining eight gifts in Paul's list.

Message/Word of Wisdom

The first gift that Paul mentions in his 1 Corinthians gift list is the **message/word of wisdom**.

The Greek word for **wisdom** in 1 Corinthians 12:8 is *sophia*.

> The Greek lexicon definition for *sophia* used in 1 Corinthians 12:8 is *the capacity to understand and function accordingly.*

Wisdom/sophia, prefaced by *logos/word*, as in **message/word of wisdom**, would indicate that the wisdom is being expressed in some way, most likely by an oral utterance as in a proclamation of wisdom.

THOUGHTS FROM THE EXPERTS ABOUT: THE WORD OF WISDOM

- A message from the Holy Spirit applying God's Word or wisdom to a specific situation.[2]

- A message or an oral communication that is full of wisdom or characterized by wisdom.[3]

- "All true words of wisdom will reflect God's plans, purposes, and ways of accomplishing things... Teaching, seeking divine guidance, counseling,

2. Arrington and Stronstad, *Full Life Bible Commentary*, 788.
3. Fee, *The First Epistle to the Corinthians*, 592.

and addressing practical needs in church government and administration may offer occasions for a word of wisdom."[4]

- A supernatural gift in which there is the sense of the divine rather than mere human experience. It implies a message given through a direct operation of the Holy Spirit at a given moment, rather than a permanent supernatural wisdom.[5]

- A spoken message that applies the use of wisdom to interpreting dreams, giving sage advice, managing affairs, using prudence in dealing with those outside the church, having skill and discretion in imparting Christian truth, defending Christ's cause, or interpreting Scripture.[6]

Read Acts 6:8–10.

What do these verses say about the wisdom of Stephen?

_____

_____

_____

Read 1 Corinthians 2:4–5.

What do these verses say about the wisdom with which Paul spoke to the Corinthians?

_____

_____

_____

_____

_____

_____

Godly wisdom encompasses understanding without reason or fact to substantiate its claims.

4. Lim, *Spiritual Gifts*, 71.

5. Donald Gee, rev. ed. *Concerning Spiritual Gifts* (Springfield, MO: Gospel Publishing House, 1972), 22–26.

6. Pearlman, *Knowing the Doctrines of the Bible,* 321–322.

Life Scenario

Fred, a new Christian, prays earnestly and daily searches the Scriptures for God's direction. God often reveals things to him through his daily devotions. Fred shares his newfound insights with other Christians. His friends are excited for him and encourage him in his search for God's truth.

Recently Fred began interspersing his conversation with the words "God told me." At first no one was too concerned, but as time went on, Fred began to use the phrase more frequently. People began to wonder what things God had actually spoken to Fred and what things were revealed to Fred in a more general sense through Scripture.

Do you think it would be a good idea to talk with Fred about his terminology? Why or why not?

_____

_____

_____

_____

_____

Write your own definition of the *message of wisdom*.

_____

_____

_____

_____

Message/Word of Knowledge

The Greek term for the **word of knowledge** in 1 Corinthians 12:8 is ***gnosis***.

The Greek Lexicon Definition for ***gnosis*** used in 1 Corinthians 12:8 is *comprehension or intellectual grasp of something.*

THOUGHTS FROM THE EXPERTS ABOUT: WORD OF KNOWLEDGE

- "The manifestation of this gift would not be the product of study as such, but God's special word through the teacher, helping to communicate a scriptural truth needed by the church...It is often dropped into the midst of a prepared lesson in such a way as to bring the truth home to those listening."[7]

- A message from the Holy Spirit revealing knowledge about people, circumstances, or biblical truth.[8]

- Revelation from God about people, circumstances, or biblical truth.[9]

- A supernaturally inspired spoken message involving facts such as things pertaining to the knowledge of God and the Christian faith, moral wisdom for right living, knowledge of Christian and Divine things involving false teachers, relations with others, and Christian duties.[10]

Read Luke 2:25–33 concerning Jesus's circumcision and presentation to the Lord.

What message of knowledge was revealed by Simon through the Spirit in this Scripture passage?

_____

_____

_____

Life Scenario

Kaitlin has invited Peggy to church many times, but this is the first time Peggy has accepted the invitation; however, as Peggy sat in the church service she felt as if the pastor was speaking directly to her. At times, he seemed to be describing in great detail the things that were happening in her life.

---

7. Lim, *Spiritual Gifts*, 73.

8. Arrington and Stronstad, *Full Life Bible Commentary*, 788.

9. Wayne H. House, *Charts of Christian Theology & Doctrine* (Grand Rapids, MI: Zondervan, 1992), 72.

10. Pearlman, *Knowing the Doctrines of the Bible*, 322.

Peggy confronted Kaitlin after the service. She was offended that Kaitlin would talk to her pastor about Peggy's personal life. Kaitlin assured Peggy that she had not talked to her pastor about Peggy.

How can Kaitlin explain to Peggy about what happened in the church service?

_____

_____

_____

_____

_____

_____

Write your own definition for the *message of knowledge*.

_____

_____

_____

_____

Some Bible scholars see a distinction in the gifts of "message/word of knowledge" and "message/word of wisdom." Others feel that the differences are not easily distinguished. David Lim says that, in general, knowledge tells us what, while wisdom tells us how, and that we need both from God.[11]

Although the gifts are closely related, a person with the "gift of knowledge" might be described as one who gives information, while a person with the "gift of wisdom" might be defined as one who gives advice or direction—applied knowledge. The two gifts often go together and may both be expressed by the same person. A pastor once said that God gave him knowledge in knowing whom he was supposed to marry, but he had to pray for wisdom in knowing how to pursue her!

---

11. Lim, *Spiritual Gifts*, 72.

Do you think there is a relationship between the gifts of message/word of wisdom and message/word of knowledge? Is so, what is that relationship?

_____

_____

_____

_____

_____

Life Thoughts

Limping toward the front of the church, I responded to an invitation given by a visiting minster to pray for anyone who would like to be healed. Experiencing a lot of pain in my leg due to an injury, I was anxious to get some relief.

However, before praying for my healing the minister surprised me by speaking to me about a different subject. He talked to me about a great deal of emotional pain I had received in the past at the hands of a minister. Not only was what he said true, but the painful experiences were still recent enough to remain raw in my thinking. Since the minster had no way of knowing what had happened, my interest was immediately peaked. A bit skeptical at first, I wondered if he had taken a wild swing and somehow inadvertently hit the nail on the head. I think what convinced me most, however, was the compassion that I felt in the next words that he spoke. He told me that on the behalf of other ministers and himself, he apologized to me for what had been done. I was amazed. Somehow God spoke through this man, giving him knowledge about my situation and wisdom to know how I could be comforted.

Walking away (without a limp), I realized my healing had come in more ways than one. God had physically healed me from the injury to my leg, but more importantly, he showed me he was also concerned about the wound that needed healing in my heart.

Gift of Faith

The Greek word for **faith** in 1 Corinthians 12:9 is *pistis*.

> The Greek lexicon definition for *pistis* used in 1 Corinthians 12:9 is *trust, belief, a special gift of faith that belongs to a select few, an unquestioning belief in God's power to aid people with miracles.*

THOUGHTS FROM THE EXPERTS ABOUT: THE GIFT OF FAITH

- Special trust in the Lord.[12]

- "The gift of faith is the ability to envision what needs to be done and trust God to accomplish it even though it seems impossible to most people."[13]

- Trusting God implicitly to perform unusual deeds.[14]

- The gift of faith is different than the faith expected of all Christians. It is an extraordinary faith which is sometimes referred by older theologians as the "faith of miracles." It is evident in times of crisis or when faith beyond the ordinary is needed.[15]

- "The gift of faith is not the saving faith every Christian has, but rather the special gift of mountain-moving faith."[16]

Read Hebrews 11:1.

What definition of faith does this verse give?

_____

_____

12. John F. Walvoord, "The Holy Spirit and Spiritual Gifts" *Bibliotheca sacra* vol. 143, no. 560 (Ap-Je 1986): 111.
13. Malphurs, *Maximizing Your Effectiveness*, 49.
14. House, *Charts of Christian Theology & Doctrine*, 73.
15. Gee, *Concerning Spiritual Gifts*, 35–36.
16. Grossmann, *There Are Other Gifts than Tongues*, 84.

Read Hebrews 11:6.

What is the difference between having the gift of faith and having the kind of faith that all believers should have, which is mentioned in Hebrew 11:6?

_____

_____

_____

_____

_____

Read Acts 6:1–8 concerning the seven men chosen to serve the day-to-day needs of the people.

How was Stephen described in verse 5?

_____

_____

What does verse 8 say was accomplished through the ministry of Stephen?

_____

_____

_____

We have been called to a present-active-participle walk of faith, not a park 'n' ride.
BETH MOORE

Life Scenario

Jonathan, known for having a strong faith in God, believes God will protect him and take care of his needs. He never worries about locking the doors of his house and car, and doesn't bother to wear a helmet when he rides his motorcycle. Jonathan trusts God completely to protect both his property and himself.

Do you think Jonathan's actions reflect the gift of faith? Why or why not?

_____

_____

_____

_____

_____

Write your own definition for the *gift of faith*.

_____

_____

_____

_____

Life Thoughts

Moving to another state can be a difficult transition, and our move from Michigan to Florida was no exception. Our daughter Kaitlin, who was in middle school, was at that difficult age where it is hard to be up-rooted. It was important to us that Kaitlin find good friends.

I noticed that during this time Kaitlin became very attached to her bird "Snuggles." I was thankful that she had a familiar friend that could make the transition with her, so you can imagine my dismay when Snuggles became sick and began to take a turn for the worse.

Although it might seem like a silly thing to many people, I requested prayer for Snuggles in a small group setting at church. You can imagine my surprise, however, when the woman who prayed did not pray for Snuggles's healing, but that our daughter would be comforted when her bird died. I felt angry and betrayed. I questioned how we could have faith enough for the healing of people if we didn't have faith enough for the healing of a bird!

Snuggles eventually died, and although God did comfort Kaitlin in the situation, the incident made me think about how important faith is. I realized that if I could not believe for the little things, I would never have the faith Jesus referred to as being capable of moving mountains.

Gifts of Healings

The Greek word for **healing** in 1 Corinthians 12:9 is *iama*.

> The Greek lexicon definition for *iama* used in 1 Corinthians 12:9 is *healing*.

THOUGHTS FROM THE EXPERTS ABOUT: THE GIFTS OF HEALINGS

- Restoring someone to physical health by divinely supernatural means.[17]

- "The gift of healing is the special ability that God gives to certain members of the body of Christ to serve as human intermediaries through whom it pleases God to cure illness and restore health apart from the use of natural means."[18]

- "This gift enables Christians to serve as God's instruments for restoring the health of others without the aid of medical tools."[19]

- "The gift of healing is the ability to intervene in a supernatural way as an instrument for the curing of illness and the restoration of health."[20]

Read Luke 9:1–2.

What kind of power and authority did Jesus give to the disciples?

_____

_____

_____

17. Arrington and Stronstad, *Full Life Bible Commentary*, 788.
18. Wagner, *Your Spiritual Gifts Can Help Your Church Grow*, 261.
19. Schwarz, *The 3 Colors of Ministry*, 128.
20.   Flynn, *19 Gifts of the Spirit*, 170.

Read Acts 28:7–9.

How was Paul used to administer healing while he was shipwrecked on the island of Malta?

_____

_____

_____

_____

Because the words ***charismata iamata*/gifts of healings** are plural in 1 Corinthians 12:9, some scholars believe the gifts of healings mentioned in this Scripture passage refer both to physical healings and emotional and mental healings.

Write your own definition for the *gifts of healings.*

_____

_____

_____

_____

Gift of Miracles

The Greek word for **miracles** in 1 Corinthians 12:10 is ***dunameis***.

> The Greek lexicon definition for ***dunameis*** used in 1 Corinthians 12:10 is *a deed that exhibits ability to function powerfully, deed of power, miracle, wonder.*

THOUGHTS FROM THE EXPERTS ABOUT: THE GIFT OF MIRACLES

- The gift of miracles covers all kinds of supernatural activities including and beyond the healing of the sick.[21]

- Being able to perform works of power.[22]

---

21. Fee, *The First Epistle to the Corinthians*, 594.
22. House, *Charts of Christian Theology & Doctrine*, 73.

- Presumably all healings are demonstrations of miraculous powers, but not all miraculous powers are healings. Miraculous powers may include exorcisms, miracles of nature, and other displays of divine power.[23]

- "The gift of miracles is the special ability that God gives to certain members of the body of Christ to serve as human intermediaries through whom it pleases God to perform powerful acts that are perceived by observers to have altered the ordinary course of nature."[24]

Read Acts 20:7–12.

What miracle was performed in this Scripture passage?

_____

_____

Read Acts 12:5–11

What miracle occurred in answer to the prayers of the Church?

_____

_____

Read Acts 19:11–12.

In this Scripture passage, the healings from diseases and evil spirits performed through the hands of Paul are referred to as miracles/*dunameis*. Do you think that healings could also be considered miracles? Do you think that there might be some overlap in the gifts that Paul mentions such as in the gifts of healings and miracles? Why or why not?

_____

_____

_____

_____

_____

---

23. D. A. Carson, *Showing the Spirit: A Theological Exposition of 1 Corinthians 12–14* (Grand Rapids, MI: Baker Books, 1987), 40.

24. Wagner, *Your Spiritual Gifts Can Help Your Church Grow*, 261.

Life Scenario

Paula, facing some tough financial times, wondered how she would pay the expenses to have her car repaired. Because Paula needed the car for her work, she paid for the repairs; however, in doing so, she ended up being $205 short in her rent payment. Paula prayed, and the day before her rent payment was due, she received a check for $205 in the mail from a friend who said she wanted to "bless" Paula. Paula had not told anyone about her circumstances.

Paula later told her friend, Phil, about the "miracle." Phil did not think this was a miracle because the problem had been solved by human intervention rather than by supernatural means.

What do you think? Would you consider Paula's $205 check a miracle? Why or why not?

_____

_____

_____

_____

Write your own definition for the *gift of miracles*.

_____

_____

_____

_____

At the end of our prayers, we say 'Amen,' which means 'so be it.' It signifies the end of a prayer. But the end of a prayer is always just the beginning. It's the beginning of a dream. It's the beginning of a miracle. It's the beginning of a promise.
MARK BATTERSON

Distinguishing Between Spirits

The Greek word for **distinguishing** (some translations say **discernment**) in 1 Corinthians 12:10 is *diakrisis*.

> The Greek lexicon definition for *diakrisis* used in 1 Corinthians 12:10 is *the ability to distinguish and evaluate. In this case, the distinguishing would involve spirit beings.*

The Greek word for **spirits** in 1 Corinthians 12:10 is *pneumata*.

> The Greek lexicon definition for **pneumata** used in 1 Corinthians 12:10 is *spirit beings or powers.*

The **gift of distinguishing between spirits** involves determining whether the spirit is from God or of another kind of power.

THOUGHTS FROM THE EXPERTS ABOUT: DISTINGUISHING BETWEEN SPIRITS

- "The gift of discernment is part of God's providential protection against error. It can express itself on a natural level by enabling Christians to distinguish between truth and deception. It can also provide them with insight into the deepest sources of truth and deception, thus entering into the supernatural realm."[25]

- Ability to judge whether or not prophecies and oral messages are from the Holy Spirit.[26]

- Distinguishing the power by which a teacher or prophet speaks. It may be instrumental in exposing false prophets.[27]

Read Acts 13:6–12.

How do you think that Paul knew the nature of the spirit within Elymas?

_____

_____

_____

_____

_____

What was the result of this encounter (verses 11–12)?

_____

_____

_____

_____

25. Schwarz, *The 3 Colors of Ministry*, 126.
26. Arrington and Stronstad, *Full Life Bible Commentary*, 789.
27. House, *Charts of Christian Theology & Doctrine*, 73.

Read Acts 16:16–18.

How do you think that Paul knew that the girl who was professing that Paul and his companions were "servants of the Most High God" was not of the Spirit of God?

_____

_____

_____

_____

Write your own definition for the *gift of distinguishing of spirits*.

_____

_____

_____

_____

> *Some people think they have discernment when actually they are just suspicious. There is a true gift of the Spirit called discerning of spirits. (1 Corinthians 12:10 KJV.) It discerns good and bad, not just bad.*
>
> **JOYCE MEYER**

Different Kinds of Tongues

The last two gifts listed in Paul's 1 Corinthians list are **different kinds of tongues** and **interpretation of tongues**. The Greek word for **tongues** in 1 Corinthians 12:10 in both of these gifts is *glossai*.

> The Greek lexicon definition for *glossai* is *a body of words and systems that makes up a distinctive language.* In 1 Corinthians 12:10, it refers to *an utterance outside the normal patterns of intelligible speech and therefore requiring special interpretation.*

THOUGHTS FROM THE EXPERTS ABOUT: THE GIFT OF TONGUES

- Speaking in a language not understood by the speaker.[28]

- A power of more or less ecstatic speech, in languages with which the speaker is not familiar. The purpose of these messages of the Spirit is to maintain the orderly use of the gifts in the public worship. When used

---

28. House, *Charts of Christian Theology & Doctrine*, 73.

with interpretation of tongues they provide the equivalent to prophecy by which the Holy Spirit can speak to the church.[29]

- "The gift of tongues is the gift of a supernatural utterance in one or more languages unknown to the speaker."[30]

- The gift of speaking supernaturally in a language never learned by the speaker in ecstatic praise addressed to God alone or as a definite message for the church.[31]

Interpretation of Tongues

The Greek word for **interpretation** in 1 Corinthians 12:10 is **hermeneia**.

The Greek lexicon definition for **hermeneia** is *the capacity of doing translation, product of interpretative procedure, interpretation or exposition of words.*

THOUGHTS FROM THE EXPERTS ABOUT: INTERPRETATION OF TONGUES

- The gift of interpretation of tongues has the same purpose as natural interpretation from one language to another, yet is different in its mode of operation because it is supernatural and comes directly from the Holy Spirit wherein the words are given by revelation.[32]

- To articulate for the community what the tongues-speaker has said. It is a Spirit-inspired oral message or word that may be given either to the tongues-speaker or to another.[33]

- "The gift of interpretation is the special ability that God gives to certain members of the Body of Christ to make known in the vernacular the message of one who speaks in tongues."[34]

- The same Holy Spirit who inspired the speaking in other tongues, whereby the words are expressed through the spirit rather than the intellect,

---

29. Gee, *Concerning Spiritual Gifts*, 57–59.

30. David K. Bernard, *Spiritual Gifts: A Practical Study with Inspirational Accounts of God's Supernatural Gifts to His Church* (Hazelwood, MO: Word Aflame Press, 1956), 185.

31. Pearlman, *Knowing the Doctrines of the Bible*, 326.

32. Gee, *Concerning Spiritual Gifts*, 62–63.

33. Fee, *The First Epistle to the Corinthians*, 598–599.

34. Wagner, *Your Spiritual Gifts Can Help Your Church Grow*, 235.

is able to inspire the interpretation as well. It is inspirational, ecstatic, and spontaneous.[35]

Read 1 Corinthians 14:26–28.

In this Scripture passage, what guidelines does Paul give for the use of the gifts of tongues and interpretation of tongues in the church?

_____

_____

_____

_____

What problems might arise in a church worship setting where Paul's guidelines are not followed?

_____

_____

_____

_____

_____

_____

There is no limit to what God can do through you, provided you do not seek your own glory.
OSWALD CHAMBERS

Write your own definition for the *gifts of tongues* and the *interpretation of tongues*.

_____

_____

_____

_____

_____

_____

_____

_____

---

35. Pearlman, *Knowing the Doctrines of the Bible,* 327.

As we will see in Lesson Five, not everyone agrees concerning the use of these gifts in today's church. Be open to the leading of the Holy Spirit in the use of the gifts God has already given to you, and be willing to use any gifts that he might give to you in the future.

Throughout the week, pray that God will give you a greater understanding of the meaning of the gifts mentioned in 1 Corinthians chapter 12, as well as an understanding of your part in the implementation of the gifts within the body of Christ.

Lord, I pray...

_____

_____

_____

_____

_____

_____

_____

_____

_____

_____

_____

_____

_____

_____

Lesson Five
Are All Gifts for Today?

An ongoing debate in the church of today regarding gifts is the question of whether or not all the gifts in the New Testament church are operational today or if some gifts were only evident during the time of the apostles.

Cessationist

Cessationists believe there are some gifts no longer available to the church today and that they ceased at some point during the time of the apostles or shortly thereafter. Differences of opinion exist as to which gifts have and have not ceased. Some Cessationists think such gifts as apostles, prophets, discernment, words of wisdom and knowledge, faith, miracles, healings, and tongues and interpretation have ceased. Other Cessationists, although cautious in their assessment, are more open to the possibility that some of these gifts might be evident in today's church.

Early twentieth-century theologian and Cessationist Benjamin B. Warfield believed there was no doubt the apostles of the early church possessed divine [gifts] *charismata*. He thought the number and variety of gifts during the apostolic age was considerable. Warfield believed further that these gifts of the early church extended to those extraordinary gifts of healings, working of miracles, prophecy, discerning of spirits, kinds of tongues, and the interpretation of tongues mentioned in 1 Corinthians 12. According to Warfield, in regard to the early church, the exception would not be a church *with* but a church *without* such gifts.[1] Warfield also maintained, however, that these gifts were distinctively for the authentication of the apostles and were only part of the credentials of the apostles as the authoritative agents of God in the founding of the church. He believed the function of the gifts was confined distinctively to the apostolic church, and they passed away with it.[2]

Cessationist and theologian Richard B. Gaffin Jr. doesn't hold to the view that all gifts have ceased or that the church does not hold any gifts today, nor does he

---

1. Benjamin B. Warfield. *Counterfeit Miracles* (1918 Reprint, London: The Banner of Truth Trust, 1972), 5–6.
2. Ibid., 6.

argue that miracles have ceased entirely or that God does not miraculously heal in the present. Gaffin believes healings do occur in today's church; however, he contends the manifestations are in response to the prayers of the people rather than specific gifts of healings and miracles such as those listed in 1 Corinthians 12:9–10.[3]

Pentecostal

Pentecostals have their modern day roots in the Pentecostal revival that began in the early 1900s. They believe salvation comes through the atonement and that Christians are justified by grace through faith and by the regeneration and renewal of the Holy Spirit. Pentecostals, in a broad sense, are Evangelical, but are distinct from some mainline Evangelical denominations based on their ideas about what is referred to as the "baptism of the Holy Spirit," which they believe is an experience that is subsequent to salvation. Pentecostals contend this "baptism" is an empowering experience that is based on the upper room episode of the early church in which believers continued, with one accord, in supplication (Acts 1:11–14), waiting for the fulfillment of the promised power that would be given to them by the Holy Spirit (Acts 1:8). Pentecostals maintain this promise was fulfilled in Acts 2:1–4:

> When the day of Pentecost came, they were all together in one place. [2] Suddenly a sound like the blowing of a violent wind came from heaven and filled the whole house where they were sitting. [3] They saw what seemed to be tongues of fire that separated and came to rest on each of them. [4] All of them were filled with the Holy Spirit and began to speak in other tongues as the Spirit enabled them.

Many Pentecostals think speaking in tongues is evidence of the baptism of the Holy Spirit. They believe this empowering experience is available for all believers today.

Pentecostals also believe there's another use for tongues, which they refer to as the *gift of tongues*. In contrast to the baptism of the Holy Spirit, which is an individual experience that may be experienced by all believers, Pentecostals feel the gift of tongues is not available to all believers, but is considered to be a "grace" *gift/charisma* given to select believers. According to Pentecostals, the gift of tongues is used for public edification of the body of Christ when used with

Let the peace of Christ rule in your hearts, since as members of one body you were called to peace. And be thankful. Let the message of Christ dwell among you richly as you teach and admonish one another with all wisdom through psalms, hymns, and songs from the Spirit, singing to God with gratitude in your hearts.
COLOSSIANS 3:15–16

---

3. Wayne Grudem, ed. *Are Miraculous Gifts for Today: Four Views.* (Grand Rapids, MI: Zondervan Publishing House, 1996), 41–42.

the gift of interpretation of tongues. Pentecostals believe the gifts of tongues and interpretation of tongues exist today. Some Pentecostals feel all the gifts of the Holy Spirit mentioned in the New Testament during the time of the apostles are available to the believer today, while others think some gifts, such as the gifts of prophet and apostle, may have ceased or have capacities differing from those in the early church.

Charismatic

The historic Charismatic renewal can be traced back to the 1960s and 1970s. The movement is known for its acceptance of speaking in tongues, healings, miraculous gifts, and prophecy. Charismatics exist within both Catholic and Protestant churches and they have no distinct theology outside their respective denominations. For the most part, Charismatics believe that the gifts, just as they were during the time of the apostles, are for the church today.

Third Wave

In the 1980s, a renewal movement called the Third Wave began to gain prominence. This term, Third Wave, was coined by Dr. C. Peter Wagner, a missions professor from Fuller Seminary, and taught by John Wimber, founder of the Association of Vineyard Churches. Wagner refers to the Pentecostal movement at the turn of the nineteenth century as the *first wave* of the Holy Spirit. The *second wave* of the Holy Spirit, as seen by Wagner, was the Charismatic movement that emerged around the middle of the twentieth century. The *third wave* renewal, which began in the 1980s and continues today, is accompanied by signs, wonders, and miracles. Wagner, who does not consider himself a Pentecostal or Charismatic, simply views himself as open to the Holy Spirit working through individuals in the church in any way God chooses.[4] Wagner feels that gifts are functional in the church today.

Commonalities

Although there are distinct and significant differences between the Cessationist, Third Wave, Pentecostal, and Charismatic, theologian Wayne Grudem believes the three have much in common. According to Grudem, all three movements (1) agree to a commitment to Scripture—recognizing Scripture as

How good and pleasant it is when God's people live together in unity!
PSALM 133:1

---

4. C. Peter Wagner, *The Third Wave of the Holy Spirit.* (Ann Arbor, MI: Vine Books Servant Publications, 1988), 18–19.

WHAT ARE SPIRITUAL GIFTS?

the inerrant Word of God and absolute authority in all matters; (2) recognize their fellowship in Christ—acknowledging that the body of Christ transcends doctrinal differences; (3) understand the importance of experiencing a personal relationship with God including prayer, worship, and hearing the voice of God through Scripture; and (4) have a measure of agreement on specific details about miracles and the work of the Holy Spirit—believing God does heal and work miracles today, guides us by the Holy Spirit, empowers us for various kinds of ministry, and, in His sovereignty, brings to our minds specific things that meet the need of the moment.[5]

For the most part, theologians and scholars within the Cessationist, Pentecostal, Charismatic, and Third Wave movements agree that, despite the variations in belief, the commonalities in these groups of believers far outweigh the differences. Although the various groups differ in their definition of some gifts, the church is united in its purpose—the unifying of the body of Christ.

Life Thoughts

A common question asked by new Christians is why, if we all believe in the same God, are there so many differences in what we believe? I was recently asked this question again and to be honest with you, I didn't have any better answer than the last time I was asked. I attempted to explain the difficulties in translating an ancient language into a modern day language. I gave an example of a particularly controversial Scripture and the reasons for the differences of interpretation. We discussed the nuances of meaning in our own language and how difficult it might be to understand an ancient language where we do not understand the circumstances surrounding what is being said.

When I was finished, my friend nodded and I smiled, but I am not sure either of us really understood. I knew that my answer was not really an answer at all, but a feeble attempt to give some kind of "mature Christian" response.

I continue to ask myself this same question. Why isn't Scripture plainer and why can't God just let us know what He means? How can we know whose interpretation is right? Perhaps the solution lies not so much in coming to a perfect understanding, but in acknowledging and understanding the differing ideas of others.

5. Grudem, *Are Miraculous Gifts for Today*, 341–342.

What do you think?

Do you believe an individual can possess gifts that appear more visibly and audibly "miraculous" such as prophecy, healing, tongues, and interpretation of tongues today, or do you think these gifts were associated exclusively with the time of the apostles? Why or why not?

_____

_____

_____

_____

_____

Life Scenario

A visiting minister came to Mt. Hope Church. He mentioned other church services where God had healed people as he prayed for them, and he invited people to come to the front of the church for prayer at the end of the church service.

Roy limped toward the front of the church after the church service. He had contacted polio when he was younger and had never quite recovered, which left him with a permanent limp. The minister sat Roy in a chair and pulled on his legs as he prayed. After a few minutes, he said that, right before his eyes, the short leg had grown. The congregation rejoiced, but then fell silent as Roy limped back toward his seat.

Do you think Roy's short leg had grown? Why or why not?

_____

_____

_____

_____

_____

_____

> *I continue to dream and pray about a revival of holiness in our day that moves forth in mission and creates authentic community in which each person can be unleashed through the empowerment of the Spirit to fulfill God's creational intentions.*
>
> **JOHN WESLEY**

Do you believe that false claims to the "miraculous" exist in today's church? What, if any, problems or abuses have you observed in the gifts of the miraculous in the church?

_____

_____

_____

_____

_____

_____

Another concern pertaining to gifts of a more visibly and audibly miraculous nature is that these gifts might at times be given a greater preeminence than other gifts of a less obviously miraculous nature. Some think there is a tendency for Christians to over-stress those gifts that appear to be more miraculous by not encouraging or even disregarding gifts that are less pronounced.

Do you think some gifts are viewed with a higher regard than others? Why or why not?

_____

_____

_____

_____

_____

_____

_____

More 1 Corinthians 12 Gifts

After the listing of Paul's gifts in 1 Corinthians 12:8–10, and after a discussion on the body of Christ in this same chapter, Paul gives another short list of gifts.

Fill in the blanks with Paul's 1 Corinthians 12:28 gift list. Depending on the translation you are using, the wording of the verse might be slightly

different from the outline below. When you are finished, you should have listed eight gifts.

1 Corinthians 12:28

> ²⁸ *And God has placed in the church first of all* _____, *second* _____, *third* _____, *then* _____, *then gifts of* _____, *of* _____, *of* _____, *and of different kinds of* _____.

Some of the gifts in this 1 Corinthians 12:28 gift list are repeated gifts from Paul's lists in Romans 12:6–8 and 1 Corinthians 12:8–10. Three of the gifts, however, were not previously mentioned. These gifts are as follows: apostle, helps, administration/guidance.

Gift of Apostle

As mentioned earlier, not all Christians affirm that the gift of **apostle** exists in the church today.

The Greek word for **apostle** in 1 Corinthians 12:28 is ***apostolos***.

> The Greek lexicon definition for ***apostolos*** used in 1 Corinthians 12:28 is *messenger, delegate, envoy.*

THOUGHTS FROM THE EXPERTS ABOUT: THE GIFT OF APOSTLE

- One who speaks authoritatively about faith and practice and was an eye-witness of the resurrected Christ.[6]

- Individuals with unusual authority who were channels of divine revelation. Apostles often had the gift of prophecy as well as that of working miracles. They were in the inner circle of the original twelve apostles and were eyewitness of the resurrection of Christ, or like Paul, had a subsequent revelation. They were limited to the first century.[7]

---

6. House, *Charts of Christian Theology & Doctrine*, 72.
7. Walvoord, "The Holy Spirit and Spiritual Gifts," 112.

- "The gift of apostle is by no means limited to the original twelve apostles. The New Testament offers examples of other men and women in apostolic ministry. An apostle's responsibility typically extends beyond his or her own local church. People with this gift distinguish themselves through their farsighted perspective."[8]

- One sent on a special mission. In the New Testament, the special mission was to preach the good news of the gospel. Today's apostolic ministry applies to anyone who has a trans-local ministry, usually leaving the pastorate to itinerate in a teaching or church planting ministry.[9]

Read Luke 6:12–16.

Jesus had many disciples; however, out of all of his disciples, Jesus chose twelve that he also called apostles. What do you think is the difference between a disciple and an apostle?

_____

_____

_____

_____

Why do you think Jesus did not designate all of his disciples as apostles?

_____

_____

_____

_____

Sometime later, Jesus sent others out to the towns where He was about to go.

God is not saving the world; It is done. Our business is to get men and women to realize it.
OSWALD CHAMBERS

---

8. Schwarz, *The 3 Colors of Ministry*, 114.

9. Edgar R. Lee, ed., *He Gave Apostles: Apostolic Ministry in the 21st Century* (Springfield, MO: Assemblies of God Theological Seminary, 2005), 16–19.

Read Luke 10:1–3.

Do you think the believers mentioned in these verses might also be called apostles? Why or why not?

_____

_____

_____

Based on the following verses, list some other New Testament Christians who were also considered apostles:

Galatians 1:19

_____

Acts 14:14

_____

Romans 16:7

_____

Do you think the gift of "apostle" was limited to the first-century church or do you believe that there are apostles today? Why or why not?

_____

_____

_____

_____

Write your own definition for the *gift of apostle.*

_____

_____

_____

_____

Life Thoughts

While listening to a Christian radio station, I heard a devotional that used the subject of "fishing" for an example. It talked about Christians being the "bait" that draws others to Christianity. I really did not connect to the fishing/bait example. I guess I don't relate to the idea of fishing at all. It is a sport for which I have neither talent nor passion.

When Jesus used the example of being "fishers of men," however, He was talking to an audience that fished for a living. It was their livelihood and they could relate to the example he was using. Jesus used examples that were easily understood by His audiences. To the disciples that fished, it was fishing. To the woman at the well, it was "living water." As we share Christ's message with others, we would do well to follow Jesus's example—speaking in a language that can be both understood and embraced.

Gift of Helps

The Greek word for **helps** in 1 Corinthians 12:28 is ***antilempseis***.

> The Greek lexicon definition for ***antilempseis*** used in 1 Corinthians 12:28 is *helpful deeds*.

THOUGHTS FROM THE EXPERTS ABOUT: THE GIFT OF HELPS

- A general term for all kinds of assistance. Some believe this gift is restricted to people serving in the office of deacon, but there is nothing to suggest that this is the case.[10]

- "...the capacity to recognize and provide assistance in meeting practical needs, thus making life a little easier for others. Often this gift concerns sacrificial, behind-the-scenes assistance and benefits others by freeing them up for vital ministers. This gift appears to be the same gift as 'service' in Romans 12:7."[11]

---

10. Carson, *Showing the Spirit*, 41.
11. Malphurs, *Maximizing Your Effectiveness*, 50.

- "The God-given special ability to serve and strengthen the body of Christ by offering others assistance in reaching goals that glorify God and strengthen the body of Christ."[12]

- The gift of helps involves assisting or lending a hand to others.[13]

Read Philippians 2:25–30.

In his letter to the Philippian church, Paul mentions his co-worker, Epaphroditus. Do you think Epaphroditus may have had the gift of helps? Why or why not?

_____
_____
_____
_____

What kinds of "jobs" might be considered gifts of helps in today's church?

_____
_____
_____
_____

Help is something that is usually appreciated, but hard to ask for.

Write your own definition for the *gift of helps*.

_____
_____
_____
_____

Life Scenario

Betty, the activities director for the church, considered her friend Millie to be a "well-rounded" person. Although Betty assigned various jobs for those helping her, she seldom gave Millie a specific assignment because

12. Rees, *S.H.A.P.E.*, 41.
13. Flynn, *19 Gifts of the Spirit*, 100.

she knew Mille could fit in wherever needed. Millie didn't understand why Betty did not give her a specific assignment. She felt that she was an extra person and not needed.

How can Betty help Millie to understand the importance of her ministry to the church?

_____

_____

_____

_____

_____

Life Thoughts

Not being particularly tech savvy, I was grateful when my friend offered to run the Powerpoint for my presentation. Although Kathleen and I had not practiced ahead of time, we got through the lecture without a hitch. In fact, I became so engrossed in what I was saying that I forgot Kathleen was helping. Somehow she anticipated when to change each slide without being prompted.

Afterward, I thanked her and told her how amazed I was that she was able to anticipate what I needed. She explained that she used to be an administrative assistant and that helping others was something at which she was good. I agreed.

Gift of Administrations/Guidance (Governments, Managing)

The Greek word for **administrations/guidance** in 1 Corinthians 12:28 is *kuberneseis*.

> The Greek lexicon definition for *kuberneseis* used in 1 Corinthians 12:28 is *administrations, governments, guidance, the ability to lead.*

The plural form of this word indicates varieties of such leading in the ecclesial body of Christ. *Kuberneseis* is a form of the Greek word *kuebernetes*, which means *governor* and is the root word for our English word *gubernatorial*.

THOUGHTS FROM THE EXPERTS ABOUT: THE GIFT OF ADMINISTRATIONS

- "The God-given special ability to serve and strengthen the body of Christ by effectively organizing resources and people in order to efficiently reach ministry goals."[14]

- Those gifted to guide and oversee the activities of the church.[15]

- "The gift of administration is the God-given ability to manage or order the affairs of a church or parachurch organization."[16]

- "The gift of administration is the special ability that God gives to certain members of the body of Christ to understand clearly the immediate and long-range goals of a particular unit of the body of Christ and to devise and execute effective plans for the accomplishment of those goals."[17]

Read Genesis 39:20–23 concerning Joseph's time as a prisoner. Do you think Joseph used administrative qualities in his work? Why or why not?

_____

_____

_____

_____

_____

_____

What examples can you think of for the gift of administration either in Bible times or today's church?

_____

_____

_____

_____

_____

_____

---

14. Rees, *S.H.A.P.E.*, 38.
15. Arrington and Stronstad, *Full Life Bible Commentary*, 1059.
16. Malphurs, *Maximizing Your Effectiveness*, 48.
17. Wagner, *Your Spiritual Gifts Can Help Your Church Grow*, 262.

Write your own definition for the *gift of administration*.

_____

_____

_____

_____

As you can see from this lesson, differing viewpoints exist concerning the definition and practice of God's gifts. Don't be discouraged if you are uncertain about the various definitions of the gifts or of their relevancy for today's church. What is most important is having the understanding that God has uniquely gifted us to work together in His kingdom.

Based on the following verse in Ephesians 1:17–18, pray that God will give you wisdom and knowledge concerning God's gifts to His people.

Lord, I pray...

¹⁷...that the God of our Lord Jesus Christ, the glorious Father, may give you the Spirit of wisdom and revelation, so that you may know him better. ¹⁸ I pray that the eyes of your heart may be enlightened in order that you may know the hope to which he has called you, the riches of his glorious inheritance in his holy people.

_____

_____

_____

_____

_____

_____

_____

_____

_____

Lesson Six
The Ephesians Gift List

The Church of Ephesus

Written to encourage Christians in their daily living, the book of Ephesians reflects upon the spiritual resources given to us through Christ. The first part of the book of Ephesians, chapters 1–3, considers the believer's calling and covers topics such as adoption, redemption, inheritance, grace, citizenship, and the love of Christ. In these chapters, Paul also introduces the idea of unity in Christ.

In the second half of the book, chapters 4–6, Paul admonishes believers to conduct themselves in a way that is worthy of their calling, and he explains God's plan to bring about unity of faith. Paul knew that the church would need to be unified itself before it could spread the message of unity to the world. In chapter four, the Scripture passage on which we will be focusing, Paul begins instructing the new believers in unity as it relates to gifts and the body of Christ. Theologian H. C. G. Moule describes Paul's discourse as passing from the revelation of doctrine to the development of practice.[1]

Ephesians, Philippians, Colossians, and Philemon are known as "prison epistles." These epistles are letters written to the churches while Paul was imprisoned at Rome (Acts 28).

Do you think the fact that Paul was imprisoned at the time that he wrote Ephesians might have influenced the way in which he wrote to the church? Why or why not?

_____

_____

_____

_____

_____

Paul, an apostle of Christ Jesus by the will of God, To God's holy people in Ephesus, the faithful in Christ Jesus: Grace and peace to you from God our Father and the Lord Jesus Christ.
EPHESIANS 1:1–2

---

1.   H. C. G. Moule, *Ephesians Studies* (Fort Washington, PA: Christian Literature Crusade, 1937), 169.

Ephesians 4 Gift List

Read Ephesians 4:7–11.

This Scripture passage, in which Paul quotes Psalm 68:18, is a somewhat perplexing passage. Not all scholars agree about what Paul is referring to in these verses. Some commentators believe the "captives" mentioned in these verses refer to those Old Testament believers who died in the faith, believing God would send the Messiah, and that these captives were subsequently led to eternal life. Others say the "captives" refer to our spiritual enemies whom Christ conquered and triumphed over at the cross. In any case, we can be assured that Christ is indeed the conqueror and that we are the beneficiaries.

What gifts does Paul mention in these verses?

_____

_____

_____

Read Ephesians 4:12–13.

What is the purpose of the gifts mentioned in this passage?

_____

_____

_____

_____

_____

What difference, if any, do you see in this gift list compared to the gift lists in Romans 12 and 1 Corinthians 12?

_____

_____

_____

_____

Ah, Sovereign LORD, you have made the heavens and the earth by your great power and outstretched arm. Nothing is too hard for you.

JEREMIAH 32:17

The Ephesians 4 gift list makes mention of the gifts in relation to the person who possesses the gift rather than referring to the gift itself. In other words, the gift to the church is *prophet* rather than *prophecy*, *teacher* rather than *teaching*, *evangelist* rather than *evangelism*, etc. In this case, the gifts are referenced in the context of their position rather than the actual enablement, and the gift to the church is the individual possessing the gift rather than the gift itself.

Do you think there is any significance to the fact that Paul lists the gifts in relation to the person or persons having the gifts rather than listing the gifts themselves? Why or why not?

_____

_____

_____

_____

_____

_____

Paul, in his numerous epistles to the churches, often pauses to give thanks for those individuals that are a gift to the church and a gift to him.

In all three of the passages we are studying, Paul associates "gifts" with grace, indicating that the gifts are graciously given; however, in the Ephesians passage, Paul uses the Greek word *domata* to refer to gifts, whereas in the Romans and 1 Corinthians passages, he refers to them as *charismata*. Paul does not explain why he chooses differing words to refer to the "gifts" mentioned in these passages. Perhaps the explanation has something to do with the inherent nature of the gifts that he references. In the Romans and 1 Corinthians passages, *charismata* are expressions of divine grace/*charis* that are not given directly *to* us, but rather these gifts, (mercy, giving, prophecy, teaching, etc.) are gifts that God administers *through* us. In the case of the Ephesians passage, however, where the gifts are mentioned in relation to the person who possesses the gift rather than referring to the gift itself (prophet rather than prophecy), the graciously given gifts (gifted individuals) do not work *through* us for the benefit of others, but are rather given *to* us and may benefit us as we prepare for ministering to others. These gifts are to be used for the body in the sense that they are given for the training of the saints in the work of the ministry. In each case, the purpose of the gifts is for God's kingdom work.

How might the gifted individuals mentioned in Ephesians 4:11 be a benefit to the body of Christ as it prepares to minister to others?

_____

_____

_____

_____

_____

Over the years, the gifts in Ephesians 4 have been given numerous designations. Some have called these gifts "office" or "ministry" gifts, while others have referred to them as "leadership" gifts. Some have even designated them as the "five-fold leadership gifts" to the church. While many Christians feel these gifts should be referred to exclusively as leadership gifts, others do not embrace such a distinction.

> *You, however, must teach what is appropriate to sound doctrine.*
> *(Paul's charge to his fellow minister, Titus)*
> **TITUS 2:1**

Theologian Anthony D. Palma believes that Paul makes a deliberate attempt to avoid distinction between clergy and laity and that any attempt to interpret the gifts as clearly defined church offices misses the point Paul wished to make, which is to show how the different functions are assigned to the various members of the body. Palma thinks these are gifts to the church that include both laity and clergy.[2]

Do you think the gifts Paul mentions in this chapter are exclusively for clergy (ministers), or do you think other Christians (laity) might also have these gifts? Why or why not?

_____

_____

_____

_____

_____

---

2. Palma, "Spiritual Gifts—Basic Considerations," 17–18.

Read Ephesians 4:11–16.

What warning does Paul give to the believers in verse 14? Why is this important?

_____

_____

_____

_____

_____

_____

How may people with the gifts of apostle, prophet, evangelist, pastor, and teacher help an individual who is confused by the destructive kinds of teachings Paul mentions in this verse?

_____

_____

_____

_____

_____

_____

_____

Ephesians 4:11 Gifts

The apostle Paul lists five gifts in his Ephesians gift list: apostle, prophet, evangelist, pastor, teacher. Because we have already discussed the gifts of **apostle**, **prophecy**, and **teaching**, which are included in the Romans and 1 Corinthians gift lists, we will concentrate on the other two gifts in Paul's Ephesians list—**evangelist** and **pastor**.

Gift of Evangelist

The Greek word for **evangelist** in Ephesians 4:11 is **_euangelistes_**.

> The Greek lexicon definition for **_euangelistes_** used in Ephesians 4:11 is _proclaimer of the gospel, bringer of good tidings._

THOUGHTS FROM THE EXPERTS ABOUT: THE GIFT OF EVANGELIST

- Those gifted in bringing new births.[3]

- Those gifted by God to proclaim the gospel to the unsaved.[4]

- "The extraordinary ability to give such a witness to the love of God as expressed in Jesus Christ that it moves others to accept that love and to become disciples of Christ."[5]

What New Testament evangelist is mentioned in Acts 21:8?

_____

What method(s) of evangelism were used by this New Testament evangelist in the following Scriptures?

Acts 8:5–8

The gospel is only good news if it gets there in time.
CARL F. H. HENRY

_____

_____

_____

_____

Acts 8:26–40

_____

_____

_____

_____

_____

In Harold Myra and Marshall Shelley's book *The Leadership Secrets of Billy Graham,* the authors describe Billy Graham, one of the greatest evangelists of the twentieth century, as being a man with a mixture of candor, awe, and love that resonated among those who worked with him. According to the authors,

---

3. Kent R. Hughes, *The Mystery of the Body of Christ* (Wheaton, IL: Crossway Books, 1990), 133.

4. Arrington and Stronstad, *Full Life Bible Commentary,* 1058.

5. Charles V. Bryant, *Rediscovering Our Spiritual Gifts: Building Up the Body of Christ Through the Gifts of the Spirit.* 6th ed. (Nashville: Upper Room Books, 1991), 72.

Billy always insisted on simply being called "Billy." Myra and Shelley believe that the title of his autobiography, *Just as I Am,* is a perfect description of his humble spirit.[6]

What qualities of character might be especially important for the ministry of evangelism?

_____

_____

_____

_____

_____

_____

Read Acts 17:1–4.

Although Paul refers to himself as an apostle, based on this Scripture, do you think he may also have the gift of an evangelist? Why or why not?

_____

_____

_____

_____

_____

Write your own definition for the *gift of evangelist*.

_____

_____

_____

_____

_____

_____

6. Harold Myra and Marshall Shelley, *The Leadership Secrets of Billy Graham* (Grand Rapids, MI: Zondervan, 2005), 15–16.

Life Thoughts

I remember my mother calling me on the phone in discouragement one day. She explained that, in her lifetime, she did not feel she was successful at "leading very many people to Christ."

I reminded my mother what the apostle Paul said in 1 Corinthians 3:6–7 concerning Christian ministry. Paul recognized that although he planted seeds, Apollos was often the one who watered the seeds, but it was God who was responsible for making the seeds grow.

I asked my mother if she had talked to anyone about God lately, and she brightened a bit as she told me that, as a matter of fact, she had talked to a lady about Jesus just yesterday. I smiled as I pictured my mother's "soul winning" efforts. I encouraged her that she, indeed, was a part of "leading many people to Christ."

Gift of Pastor

In this particular Scripture passage (Ephesians 4:11), in regards to the expression **pastors and teachers**, the definite article (the) is not repeated grammatically in the Greek as it is with the other gifts in this verse. Because of this, some theologians believe **pastor** and **teacher** are the same gift, others believe the two gifts should be considered separate gifts, and still others believe that in the context of this particular passage in Ephesians, all of the ministry offices are "teaching" offices. For the purpose of this study, and because the original language does not demand it, we will consider the terms **pastor** and **teacher** separately.

The Greek word for **pastor/shepherd** in Ephesians 4:11 is ***poimen***.

> The Greek lexicon definition for ***poimen*** used in Ephesians 4:11 is *shepherd, guardian or leader.*

In the New Testament, the Greek word ***poimen***, in the traditional sense of the word, can refer to a "shepherd" or a "sheep herder" but might also refer to a person who serves as a "guardian" or "leader." In Luke 2, the word is used in reference to those herding sheep at the time of the announcement of Christ's birth in Bethlehem. ***Poimen*** is also used in Matthew 9:36 and Mark 6:34 in describing the compassion Christ felt for the crowds, comparing them to "sheep without a shepherd." In other books of the New Testament, ***poimen*** is used metaphorically to refer to Christ himself, such as in Hebrews 13:20 where he is described as "that great shepherd of the sheep," and in 1 Peter 2:25 where he is called "the shepherd and overseer of [our] souls." The reference to ***poimen*** in our study in Ephesians 4:11 is another metaphoric example; however, in this instance it refers to a human leader or overseer and is often translated "pastor."

People of biblical times had a rural orientation and were more aware of the duties of a shepherd/sheepherder than we are in today's culture. They understood, for example, that the shepherd led the sheep.

THOUGHTS FROM THE EXPERTS ABOUT: THE GIFT OF PASTOR

- "The gift of shepherding—in contrast to the gift of counseling—involves a long-term commitment to a group of fellow Christians. Contrary to widespread opinion, this gift is not necessary for a pastor of a local church."[7]

- Those chosen and gifted to oversee the church and care for its spiritual needs. Pastors may also be referred to as elders or overseers.[8]

- Pastor means *shepherd*. Pastors are shepherds of the flock that are under their care. At times these individuals may exhibit tenderness, caring, and nurturing, but may also display resolute strength in their protection of the flock. A pastor makes feeding the sheep a top priority.[9]

- "The extraordinary ability to carry varieties of spiritual, physical, and social concerns for groups and individuals and to persist over long periods of time and circumstances with effective care-giving."[10]

In the course of time I came to realize that nothing so quieted and reassured the sheep as to see me in the field. The presence of their master and owner and protector put them at ease as nothing else could do, and this applied day and night.

PHILLIP KELLER

---

7. Schwarz, *The 3 Colors of Ministry*, 121.
8. Arrington and Stronstad, *Full Life Bible Commentary*, 1058.
9. Hughes, *The Mystery of the Body of Christ*, 133.
10. Bryant, *Rediscovering Our Spiritual Gifts*, 121.

Read the qualities of Jesus, "the Good Shepherd," in John 10:1–11.

What qualities of pastor/shepherd do you see in these verses?

_____

_____

_____

_____

_____

Can you think of a pastor who exemplified the role of pastor/shepherd? If so, what shepherd attributes did he or she convey?

_____

_____

_____

_____

Write your own definition for the *gift of pastor*.

_____

_____

_____

_____

Life Scenario

People refer to Carl as a "church planter." When Carl feels God leading him to an area that needs evangelizing, he sets to work "planting" a church. When Carl first comes to a new community, he locates a building where the church can meet. After renting the facility for Sunday morning meetings, Carl begins evangelizing the area. He enjoys going door to door to houses around the surrounding community, where he can introduce himself and invite people to church. Carl nurtures the new believers in the congregation, patiently instructing them in their newfound faith. He performs weddings and funerals, visits those that are sick and, in general, ministers to the needs of the people.

After the congregation grows and the church becomes financially stable, Carl begins work on a church building. He works with local contractors and negotiates with them about the new church construction.

But it always seems that as soon as the building is completed and things are going well, Carl senses God calling him to start another church in another community. Carl hopes someday he might complete a church building and be able to stay with that community, but it never seems to work out that way. Carl knows God has called him into ministry, but at times he wonders what kind of ministry he is involved in. Is he a pastor or evangelist, or is he perhaps an apostle?

Do you think Carl's ministry should be considered a gift? Why or why not?

_____

_____

_____

_____

_____

Dr. C. Peter Wagner comments on the office variations in today's Christian churches. He believes there are considerable differences as to which offices are recognized across denomination lines. Some churches believe only those descriptions mentioned in Ephesians 4:11 should be considered, while others add those described in the Pastoral Epistles such as elders, deacons, and bishops. Still others go beyond this and add such duties as general and district superintendent, state overseer, lieutenant, captain, etc.

Dr. Wagner admits that for some Christians this concept may be confusing, but for others it is an indication of the flexibility and creativity which he believes is the very fiber of the Christian faith. According to Wagner, the point to be remembered is that regardless of what the office is named, the person who fills that office should qualify for it based on his or her God-given gift mix.[11]

The life of trust delivers us by reminding us no individual is responsible for all the work in the world, only for a small share. I may have five, or two, or only one talent. I am to do that which I am called to do, nothing more.

HANNAH WHITALL SMITH

---

11. Wagner, *Your Spiritual Gifts Can Help Your Church Grow*, 61.

Do you think it is important for a person who holds a position in the church body to be gifted in that particular role? Why or why not?

_____

_____

_____

_____

_____

_____

Wagner believes that a frequent growth problem in American churches involves people who are allowed to occupy ecclesiastical [church] offices without the corresponding appropriate gift-mix. He believes ecclesiastical offices are often awarded on the basis of seniority, influence, personality, political manipulation, prestige or rotation.[12]

Do you think this may be a problem in today's church? Why or why not?

_____

_____

_____

_____

_____

_____

The apostle Paul made it clear that apostles, prophets, evangelists, pastors and teachers are most definitely gifts to the church. He realized, however, that those possessing these gifted roles would need the love and support of the body of Christ. In 2 Thessalonians 3:1–2, Paul asked for prayer support from the churches to which he ministered. He specifically asked the believers to:

...pray for us that the message of the Lord may spread rapidly and be honored, just as it was with you. ² And pray that we may be delivered from wicked and evil people, for not everyone has faith.

12.   Wagner, _Your Spiritual Gifts Can Help Your Church Grow_, 61.

Take some time to pray for those gifted with these special ministry gifts.

Lord, I pray...

_____

_____

_____

_____

_____

_____

_____

_____

_____

_____

Lesson Seven
Questions Concerning the Gifts

In Lessons One through Six we talked about God's gifts to believers in the early church and discussed how these gifts might be regarded in the church today. We also studied the apostle Paul's gift lists in Romans 12, 1 Corinthians 12 and Ephesians 4, and attempted to define the various gifts in these lists. In Lesson Seven, we will discuss some questions that commonly arise when studying the subject of gifts.

As we proceed in this lesson, you should answer the questions as honestly as possible. Remember that even Bible scholars do not always agree and that your ideas are important.

Where Do Gifts Come From?

Many Christians refer to the gifts listed by Paul as gifts of the Spirit, but are the gifts exclusively a manifestation of the Spirit? Where do gifts come from?

Fill in the blanks in the following Scripture passages we are studying regarding gifts and the body of Christ:

1 Corinthians 12:4–6.

> 4 There are different kinds of gifts, but the same _____ distributes them. 5 There are different kinds of service, but the same _____. 6 There are different kinds of working, but in all of them and in everyone it is the same _____ at work.

Ephesians 4:4–6

> 4 There is one body and one _____, just as you were called to one hope when you were called; 5 one _____, one faith, one baptism; 6 one _____ and Father of all, who is over all and through all and in all.

What do these Scripture passages tell us about the Trinitarian aspect of the gifts—the role of God the Father, Son, and Holy Spirit?

_____

_____

_____

_____

Look again at the verses. Highlight or circle the word *same* in 1 Corinthians 12:4–6. After completing this, highlight or circle the word *one* in Ephesians 4:4–6.

What, if anything, might be the significance of Paul's use of the words *same* and *one* in these verses?

_____

_____

_____

_____

_____

...that all of them may be one, Father, just as you are in me and I am in you. May they also be in us so that the world may believe that you have sent me. I have given them the glory that you gave me, that they may be one as we are one.

JOHN 17:21–22

Christians all belong to one body. In general, we all share the same belief in God. We are all indwelt by the same Spirit. We all share the same hope. We all serve the same Lord. We all have the same faith—belief in Christ. The Trinitarian view of God as Father, Son, and Holy Spirit, is a distinct break from the pagan polytheistic belief of many gods that was prevalent at the time of the early church.

According to theologian John Stott, Christian unity arises from the unity of our God. Stott maintains there is only one body because there is only one Spirit. There is one hope belonging to our Christian calling. There is one faith and one baptism because there is one Lord and there is one Christian family. This family embraces everyone because there is one God and Father—a God who is "above all and through all and in all" (Ephesians 4:6).[1]

_____

1. John R. Stott, *The Message of Ephesians* (Downers Grove, IL: Inter-Varsity Press, 1979), 150.

Richard Gaffin Jr. believes 1 Corinthians 12:4–6 and Ephesians 4:4–6 give a fully theological and Trinitarian perspective on the bestowal of gifts. The gifts are not only the Spirit's, but Christ's and the Father's as well. Gaffin feels this Trinitarian perspective helps to correct a tendency toward a one-sided emphasis on the Spirit in regards to the gifts and the church.[2]

Are There Other Gifts?

Today's church continues to debate whether or not Paul's gift lists are all-inclusive or whether they should be considered merely representative of the many God-given gift possibilities. Some Bible scholars think the gift lists provided by the apostle Paul in the Scriptures are most likely representative of many gift possibilities rather than being exhaustive or complete. Many feel Paul used an *ad hoc* approach, meaning that the examples of gifts Paul used in his lists were generally structured for the particular church situation that he addressed. They suppose this might have been the case in the Corinthian church for which Paul addressed problems concerning prophecy, tongues and interpretation, and how these gifts might be properly used in corporate worship.

Craig Keener, professor of New Testament, believes the gift lists of Paul are representative of many gift possibilities and that he might very well have included other gifts in his listing beyond those he listed in his epistles.[3]

Gordon Fee thinks Paul's list of gifts in 1 Corinthians 12:8–10 is *ad hoc*, and most likely reflects the Corinthian situation. Fee feels Paul's concern was more with instruction about spiritual gifts rather than with the number and kinds. He believes further that the list of nine items in 1 Corinthians 12:8–10 is neither carefully worked out nor exhaustive, but is merely *representative* of the many possibilities of the diversity of the Spirit's manifestations.[4]

Some other Christians disagree, believing that Paul's gift lists are complete. These teachers and scholars believe gifts are limited to those found in Romans 12, 1 Corinthians 12, and Ephesians 4, and that although a person may have individual characteristics such as passions, abilities, talents, and personality traits, these should not be defined as gifts.

---

2. Gaffin, *Perspectives on Pentecost*, 48–49.
3. Keener, *Gift Giver*, 114.
4. Fee, *The First Epistle to the Corinthians*, 585.

C. Peter Wagner believes the gift listings of Paul are not all-inclusive and may be expanded to include other gifts; however, he also thinks there is a distinct difference between Spirit gifts and natural talents.[5] Based on other Scripture passages, Wagner adds the gifts of *celibacy, voluntary poverty, martyrdom, hospitality, missionary, intercession,* and *exorcism* to Paul's gift lists.[6]

Read the following Scripture passages and tell what God-given enablements are included in these passages and whether or not you would consider them gifts. Explain your conclusions.

1 Chronicles 15:22

_____

_____

_____

You discover your role in life through your relationship with others.
RICK WARREN

Daniel 1:16–17

_____

_____

_____

Exodus 35:30–36:1

_____

_____

_____

_____

Life Scenario

Renee does not consider herself gifted. She recently participated in a Bible study that studied the gifts mentioned in 1 Corinthians 12, but she did not feel that she had any of the gifts discussed in this Scripture passage.

Renee talked to her friend Lorie about her frustrations regarding the fact that she did not feel "gifted." Lorie is not sure how Renee's abilities

5. Wagner, *Your Spiritual Gifts Can Help Your Church Grow,* 85.
6. Ibid., 262–263.

fit into the Bible's list of gifts, but she sees how Renee ministers to others by writing thoughtful cards and letters to church members. Renee also occasionally writes devotionals for the church's newsletter. Lorie hears many people in the church comment about how much they enjoy Renee's devotionals.

Do you think Renee's writing is a gift? Why or why not?

_____

_____

_____

_____

How can Lorie help Renee understand the importance of the writing ministry God has given to her?

_____

_____

_____

_____

_____

One dimension of spiritual growth is simply coming to terms with who we are and who we're not.
MARK BATTERSON

What do you think?

Do you believe the apostle Paul's gift lists are all-inclusive or merely representative of various "gift" possibilities? Do you think other God-given enablements should be considered gifts? Why or why not?

_____

_____

_____

_____

_____

_____

_____

_____

Do you think Paul's gift list might have included other gifts if he had lived in today's church? Why or why not?

_____

_____

_____

_____

_____

For you created my inmost being; you knit me together in my mother's womb.

PSALM 139:13

From the time we are born, God gives us unique enablements. He knew us before we were born (Psalm 139:13) and shaped us for His purposes. Some are evident from childhood, while others are more apparent after salvation. God may add to and enhance these enablements at any time according to His will. Our learning may also enhance them.

Whether you believe these enablements to be abilities, personality traits, attributes, talents, or gifts, all have the potential, after salvation, to become ministries. If we allow them to, these ministries can be used for God's purposes—the enhancement of His kingdom. All are from God and can be supernaturally empowered for His work.

Beyond the enablements that Paul included in his gift lists, make a list of any others you think might be useful in ministry.

_____

_____

_____

_____

_____

Are All Gift Manifestations from God?

Earlier in the lesson, we mentioned that "false claims" to the miraculous may exist in the church today. But what exactly are false gifts and how can we know the difference between what is truly a gift from God and what is not? In this section, we'll briefly discuss false claims regarding gifts. I want to emphasize the word *briefly* because any consideration of false manifestations can be a study in itself.

Read James 1:17.

According to this verse, what kinds of gifts come from God?

_____

The Greek word **teleios**, which is sometimes interpreted *perfect*, may refer to something that is *complete* or *whole*. The meaning of this adjective includes the ideas of *full-growth, maturity, soundness,* and *completeness*. In the context of this verse, **perfect** would refer to *something meeting the highest standard*.

What does this tell us about the gifts that come from God?

_____
_____
_____

The LORD is good, a refuge in times of trouble. He cares for those who trust in him.
NAHUM 1:7

Read Luke 11:11–13.

How can we be assured that God will give us only good gifts?

_____
_____
_____
_____

Life Thoughts

Every year the first graders at Fox Elementary School put on a production of "The Wizard of Oz." Children and parents alike look forward to this special activity. Our daughter, Alicia, was especially excited to be a part of her first play.

111

The night before casting parts, however, Alicia was worried. She was afraid she would not get the part she wanted. Her concern proved to be unfounded; the next day her name was chosen second in the class lottery when the time came for picking parts.

After her name was chosen, Alicia excitedly told her teacher that she wanted to be Toto. The teacher was surprised. In the past there had never been a Toto—at least not a human one. Normally Dorothy carried a stuffed replica of her dog around in a basket. With no more than a moment's hesitation, however, Alicia's teacher smiled and granted our daughter's wish. Alicia was ecstatic!

On the day of the play, I watched my smiling daughter, sporting the tail and ears that we had made for her, follow Dorothy around on a leash. Alicia was doing what she wanted to do, and she was very happy.

As God's children, we also can be assured that God will choose a part for us in his kingdom work that we will enjoy—and that will make us very happy.

Where Do False Gifts Come From?

Along with those good gifts that God provides, there are manifestations that may not be from God.

Read Acts 16:16–18.

How do you think Paul knew that the spirit within the girl was from the demonic realm?

_____

_____

_____

_____

Unfortunately, not all false claims to gifts are easily distinguished. The apostle Paul also speaks of some enemies of the gospel who come in human form. Paul refers to these individuals as *"false apostles, deceitful workers, masquerading as apostles of Christ"* (2 Corinthians 11:13).

What reasons might a person have for falsely claiming gifts of the miraculous?

_____

_____

_____

_____

There will always be those people in our society who intentionally deceive others for their own purposes. However, although there are many deliberate false claims to the miraculous, there are also circumstances when the error might not be intentional, but might instead be based on misunderstandings regarding the purpose and practice of gifts. This was most likely the case which Paul describes in 1 Corinthians 14, with the Corinthian church and their misuse of the gifts of tongues, interpretation, and prophecy. Paul recognized that the Corinthians were imperfect people who would, on occasion, make mistakes in the practicing of the gifts.

Life Scenario

Kyle, excited about his newfound faith, began attending church regularly. He joined a small group discussing God's gifts to the body of Christ. Kyle was intrigued about the possibility of gifts in his own life, especially those mentioned in 1 Corinthians 12: words of wisdom and knowledge, tongues and interpretation, and prophecy. One Sunday, during an extremely moving worship service at his church, Kyle spoke out during the service and began quoting an especially meaningful Scripture he read earlier in the week during his personal time of devotion.

Do you think Kyle was manifesting one of the gifts mentioned in 1 Corinthians 12? Why or why not?

_____

_____

_____

_____

By the grace God has given me, I laid a foundation as a wise builder, and someone else is building on it. But each one should build with care. For no one can lay any foundation other than the one already laid, which is Jesus Christ.

1 CORINTHIANS 3:10–11

How might you help Kyle realize the difference between the human spirit and the Spirit of God who is manifested in the gifts given to His people?

_____

_____

_____

_____

_____

_____

In some instances the correcting of false manifestations and abuses may not be easy. We should remember God gives wisdom in such cases. James describes this wisdom from above as *"pure; then peace-loving, considerate, submissive, full of mercy and good fruit, impartial and sincere"* (James 3:17). Although it is important to remember that *"our struggle is not against flesh and blood, but against the rulers, against the authorities, against the powers of this dark world and against the spiritual forces of evil in the heavenly realms"* (Ephesians 6:12), it is equally important to remember we will continue to grow in grace until the Lord returns for His church. This includes mistakes and misunderstandings we make along the way.

Keep in mind that our real enemy is not of flesh and blood. Ask God to help you have grace and mercy when dealing with any gift abuses and remember what the epistle of James says: *"If any of you lacks wisdom, you should ask God, who gives generously to all without finding fault, and it will be given to you"* (James 1:5).

Pray that God will help you to discern God's gifts from any intentional or unintentional false manifestations.

Lord, I pray...

_____

_____

_____

_____

_____

_____

_____

_____

_____

_____

_____

Lesson Eight
What Gifts Are Not

At this point in our study, you have probably formed some ideas of what you think gifts are and how they can be used in the church. Before we proceed further in our study, however, it might be a good idea to further clarify our God-given gifts by discussing "what gifts are not." Several areas of common misconceptions arise regarding the subject of gifts. In this lesson we will focus on three of these areas: (1) the difference between gifts and the fruit of the Spirit, (2) the relationship between gifts and a person's spirituality, and (3) gifts and a person's universal responsibility.

Gifts or Fruit?

Christians often confuse the *gifts* of the Spirit and what the Bible speaks of as the *fruit* of the Spirit. Although both gifts and fruit are desirable attributes for Christians, important differences exist between the two.

Fruit of the Spirit
Read Galatians 5:22–23.

What *fruit* does Paul mention in this Galatians Scripture passage?

_____

_____

_____

_____

_____

The Greek word for **fruit** in Galatians 5:22 is ***karpos***.

> The Greek lexicon definition for ***karpos*** used in Galatians 5:22 is *fruit, product or outcome of something.*

In Galatians 5, this "fruit" refers to a list of *virtues* that follow a list of *vices*. Paul refers to these vices as "acts of the sinful nature."

Read Galatians 5:19–21. How do these sinful attributes differ from the fruit of the Spirit?

_____

_____

_____

_____

_____

Read Romans 8:5.

What does this verse say about those who live according to the sinful nature as opposed to those who live in accordance with the Spirit of God?

_____

_____

_____

_____

What definition would you give for the *fruit of the Spirit*?

_____

_____

_____

_____

_____

There can be a bountiful harvest of divine fruit because of the Good Gardener's great skill and my simple, humble, hearty response to His work within.

W. PHILLIP KELLER

Life Scenario

Consider the following scenarios:

Peter, a production line supervisor, is a patient and gentle person who is kind to his fellow workers and is known as a boss that gives "second chances." When an employee fails to meet job expectations, Peter does not immediately take disciplinary action, but first discusses the situation with the employee to find out what can be done to make the job more productive.

Recently Peter was passed by for a managerial position. The employees who work with Peter think management is more interested in productivity than the circumstances and difficulties that the workers encounter on the job. They admire Peter and would like to see him promoted. Peter's supervisors, however, think he is too "soft" and that he is slow to take disciplinary action when employee expectations are not met.

What fruit might be evident in Peter's life?

_____

_____

Do you think Peter's "fruitful" attributes might be hindering his job productivity? Why or why not?

_____

_____

_____

Cara, known as a peacemaker, doesn't like conflict and is upset when she feels there is a disagreement between a co-worker and herself. Rather than push her ideas, Cara sometimes takes the "smaller piece of cake" in order to resolve tensions.

Some co-workers admire Cara's disposition. Others view her as a "doormat" and think she needs to be more assertive.

Blessed are the peacemakers, for they will be called children of God.
MATTHEW 5:9

Do you think Cara might be too compromising in her peacemaking efforts? Why or why not?

_____

_____

_____

_____

Do you think the attributes of the fruit of the Spirit are always viewed as positive virtues by non-Christians? Why or why not?

_____

_____

_____

_____

Do you think Christians can have the fruit of the Spirit and still be assertive? If so, how might this be accomplished?

_____

_____

_____

_____

_____

What differences do you see between gifts and the fruit?

_____

_____

_____

_____

_____

According to Donald Gee, a fundamental difference exists between the fruit of the Spirit and the gifts of the Spirit. Fruit is the outcome of steady growth from within and takes time to develop. Gifts, on the other hand, may be given by the generous hand of someone from without. They are immediate and complete, although when exercised by the recipient they may become more perfected by use.[1]

David Hubbard, author of *Unwrapping Your Spiritual Gifts*, believes the gifts of the Spirit have to do with *mission*, whereas the fruit of the Spirit refers to *character* and is a God-implemented means of making God's people more like him.[2]

Unlike the gifts, which are distributed to individuals as God chooses, *all* of the fruit of the Spirit are available to *all* believers and should be cultivated as such. In other words, although not all believers are expected to have all the gifts, all believers are expected to exhibit all the fruit. It is the expected outcome of Christian growth. The gifts of a person may define an individual Christian, but the fruits of the Spirit should define all Christians.

Life Scenario

Andrea, currently working as a bookkeeper for a large church in her community, is sometimes harsh in her response to people's questions and critical of their lack of understanding. Although recognizing Andrea's accounting skills, Pastor Don is concerned about the complaints his is receiving about her. Andrea says she does not have the gifts of patience and kindness.

What problems, if any do you see with Andrea's logic?

_____

_____

_____

_____

_____

_____

1. Gee, *Concerning Spiritual Gifts*, 65.

2. David Allen Hubbard, *Unwrapping Your Spiritual Gifts* (Waco, TX: Word Books Pub., 1985), 121.

What advice, if any, do you think Pastor Don should give to Andrea?

_____

_____

_____

_____

_____

_____

> *Be kind and compassionate to one another, forgiving each other, just as in Christ God forgave you.*
>
> **EPHESIANS 4:32**

Possession of the Gifts and Their Relationship to Spirituality

The second item in our list of "what gifts are not" involves the possession of gifts and their relationship with an individual's "spirituality." Unfortunately, too often we tend to judge how "spiritual" a person is by looking at the manifestation of the gifts that are present or not present in his or her life. But are the gifts a person possesses really indicative of his or her spirituality?

Read John 11:49–53.

Caiaphas, a member of the Sanhedrin, was the high priest that year. Scripture considers Caiaphas' words as a prophecy even though he did not realize what he was saying and was instrumental in the death of Jesus (Matthew 26:57–67).

Does the fact that Caiaphas prophesied indicate a level of spiritual maturity? Why or why not?

_____

_____

_____

_____

_____

_____

Life Scenario

Caleb, a new Christian, is already beginning to experience God's gifts in his life. Two of the gifts that are becoming evident in Caleb's life are the gifts of "words of wisdom" and "words of knowledge." Some of the people that attend Caleb's church think that because of these gifts, Caleb should serve on the Board of Deacons.

Do you think that Caleb should be put on the Board of Deacons based on these giftings? Why or why not?

_____
_____
_____
_____

Do you think that our God-given gifts require a spiritual level of holiness before they can be bestowed? Why or why not?

_____
_____
_____
_____

Evidence of True Spirituality

Read Matthew 7:15–20.

What do these verses say about fruit?

_____
_____
_____
_____
_____
_____
_____

Why might it be important to recognize a Christian's level of spirituality by his or her fruit rather than by his or her gifts?

_____

_____

_____

_____

_____

_____

The Bible says, *"by their fruit you will recognize them"* (Matthew 7:20). People may or may not retain the gifts God has given them independent of their relationship with Christ. Jesus said a branch cannot bear fruit unless it remains attached to the vine. In the same manner, a Christian will not continue to bear fruit if he or she does not remain connected to Christ. Perhaps the only true indicator of a person's spirituality is his or her fruit.

> *When we ask God to give us the precious fruits of His own Spirit, these are bestowed always and only through the increased presence of His own person.*
> **W. PHILLIP KELLER**

Life Thoughts

My sister-in-law, who works as a bank teller, came across a counterfeit bill one day while she was counting money at the bank. I asked her how she knew the money was counterfeit, but she didn't have an answer for me. She said she didn't know how she knew; she just did. I believe Linda knew the bill was counterfeit because she was used to working with what was genuine.

As Christians, we also can know what is counterfeit by spending time with what is real. As we read the truth of Scripture, we will be more equipped to recognize the differences.

Gifts or fruit: do you think one is more important than the other? Why or why not?

_____

_____

_____

_____

_____

Hubbard says God commands and enables us to participate in both. God wants His people to have a holy balance. A gifted individual pushing for spiritual success can come off as harsh, proud, or rash without the fruit of the Spirit. Fruit without gifts can lead to self-centeredness or isolation. Hubbard believes that neither God nor we can settle for anything less than both.[3]

Do you agree with Hubbard's assessment? Why or why not?

_____

_____

_____

_____

_____

What does Jesus' statement in John 15:4–5 say about bearing fruit?

_____

_____

_____

_____

Therefore, as God's chosen people, holy and dearly loved, clothe yourselves with compassion, kindness, humility, gentleness and patience.

COLOSSIANS 3:12

Before listing the gifts in his Ephesians 4 gift list, Paul mentions some Christ-like attributes that are important for Christians to remember while living a life worthy of the calling they have received.

Read Ephesians 4:2.

What Christ-like attributes do you see in this verse?

_____

_____

_____

_____

_____

---

3.   Hubbard, *Unwrapping Your Spiritual Gifts*, 121.

Do you see any similarities in the Ephesians 4:2 list of attributes and in the fruit of the Spirit list that Paul gives in Galatians 5:22–23 of love, joy, peace, forbearance (patience), kindness, goodness, faithfulness, gentleness, and self-control? If so, what similarities do you see?

_____

_____

_____

_____

Following is a list of fruit mentioned in Galatians 5:22–23. Write the names of Christians that you know, and/or Bible characters that show evidence of these attributes.

Fruit or Christ-like Attribute	Christian Acquaintances	Bible Characters
Love		
Joy		
Peace		
Forbearance (Patience)		
Kindness		
Goodness		
Faithfulness		
Gentleness		
Self-control		

What can you do to help cultivate fruit in your own life?

_____

_____

_____

_____

_____

_____

The Gifts of the Spirit and the Christian's Responsibility

What are our universal Christian responsibilities and how do they relate to our God-given gifts?

The third item in our list of "what gifts are not" involves the universal responsibilities of all Christians and how these obligations relate to a person's individual giftings. Some universal responsibilities apply to all Christians whether or not they are gifted in a particular area. For example, not every Christian has the gift of faith, but all Christians are expected to have faith. Not all Christians have the gift of mercy, but all Christians are expected to be merciful. In the same way, not all Christians have the gift of evangelism, but all Christians are expected to evangelize.

Read the statement made by Jesus in Matthew 28:19–20.

Who do you think is obligated to keep this commission?

_____

_____

_____

Bible scholars agree that this statement, given to the remaining eleven disciples after Jesus's ascension into heaven, is meant for all Christians. It's sometimes referred to as the "Great Commission." All believers are expected to make disciples.

Do you think the gift of evangelism mentioned in Ephesians 4:11 differs from the universal call of evangelism given to all Christians? If so, how does it differ?

_____

_____

_____

_____

_____

Because not all Christians have *the gift of evangelism* does not dismiss all believers from their duties to the Great Commission. Each believer is called to work together in the context of his or her individual gifts toward this great mission. In this sense, no believer is excluded from his or her universal Christian callings.

Life Scenario

After becoming a Christian, Randy immediately began telling others about his faith in God. He lives a life that shows he is truly a follower of Christ.

Recently, some of the people from Randy's church organized evangelism teams to do street witnessing. Randy decided not to join the witnessing teams, saying that he did not feel comfortable doing this kind of ministry. Now some of the church members are criticizing Randy saying he is not living up to the responsibilities of the "Great Commission."

Do you think Randy should have participated in the street witnessing event even though he felt uncomfortable? Why or why not?

_____

_____

_____

_____

_____

_____

Christian Schwarz talks about the danger of what he calls "gift projection." He believes Christians tend to project their gifts onto others. Schwarz gives the example of those with a gift of hospitality who cannot understand why others have so much difficulty in that area.

Schwarz believes gift projection is particularly prevalent in the area of evangelism. Many Christians with this gift deny it's a gift from God, and feel they are only doing what all Christians should be doing. In this way, they project their opinions on others, causing those without the gift of evangelism to have a guilty conscience, even though the truth is that not all Christians are gifted to reach out evangelistically in the way they themselves do.[4]

Just as it is important not to project our gifts on others, it is also crucial that a person not use their "lack of gifts" as an excuse to be disobedient to God's universal calling. Either extreme is against God's purposes—our universal calling, and our ministry within the body of Christ.

Life Thoughts

My daughter Alicia and her husband Dan love to entertain. Dan is an excellent cook and there is nothing the two of them like better than sharing a meal with friends. Guests arrive for overnight stays frequently— family, friends, missionaries passing through the area, or anyone so inclined to stop for a visit. Their home is not large, and the meals are often served around the coffee table, sometimes while guests and hosts alike are seated on the floor; however, no one seems to mind.

One of the reasons I recognize this special knack for hospitality in Dan and Alicia is because it is something that I myself do not possess. Although I enjoy spending time with our friends, entertaining for me proves to be an effort. I don't enjoy cooking, and getting things ready for company does not always come easily. I have come to recognize this special part of my daughter and son-in-law while understanding that I am good at other things.

---

4. Schwarz, *The 3 Colors of Ministry*, 97.

Write a prayer asking God to strengthen you to be obedient to all God has called you to do. Pray that you will not be judgmental or critical regarding the calling of other Christians.

Lord, I pray...

_____

_____

_____

_____

_____

_____

_____

_____

_____

_____

_____

Lesson Nine
The Purpose of Gifts

Part of the process of defining our God-given gifts involves gaining an understanding of their purpose. It is hard to imagine that not only does God have a plan for His church, but He has chosen us, as individuals, to be a part of that plan.

Up until now, some of the topics covered concerning gifts have been controversial. Not all Bible scholars and teachers agree regarding the number of gifts available to believers or even what these individual gifts may entail. Concerning the *purpose* of the gifts, however, Christians are much more in agreement, and although the apostle Paul may have had different reasons for his teachings on the gifts depending on the particular church to which he was speaking and the specific circumstances, some very distinct commonalities in purpose were important to the churches in Rome, Ephesus, and Corinth, and are equally paramount to the church today.

Fill in the blanks from these Scripture passages concerning gifts. Your answers may vary slightly depending on the Bible translation that you are using, but the meaning will be essentially the same.

Romans 12:4–5

> *⁴ For just as each of us has one _____ with many _____,*
> *and these _____ do not all have the same function, ⁵ so in*
> *Christ we, though many, form one _____, and each _____*
> *belongs to all the others.*

Ephesians 4:11–16

> *¹¹ So Christ himself gave the apostles, the prophets, the evangelists, the*
> *pastors and teachers, ¹² to equip his people for works of service, so that*
> *the _____ of Christ may be built up ¹³ until we all reach unity in the*
> *faith and in the knowledge of the Son of God and become mature, at-*
> *taining to the whole measure of the fullness of Christ. ¹⁴ Then we will no*

longer be infants, tossed back and forth by the waves, and blown here and there by every wind of teaching and by the cunning and craftiness of people in their deceitful scheming. *15* Instead, speaking the truth in love, we will grow to become in every respect the mature body of him who is the head, that is, Christ. *16* From him the whole _____, joined and held together by every supporting ligament, grows and builds itself up in love, as each _____ does its work.

1 Corinthians 12:12–20

12 Just as a _____, though one, has many _____, but all its many _____ form one _____, so it is with Christ. *13* For we were all baptized by one Spirit so as to form one _____—whether Jews or Gentiles, slave or free—and we were all given the one Spirit to drink. *14* Even so the _____ is not made up of one _____ but of many.

15 Now if the foot should say, "Because I am not a hand, I do not belong to the _____," it would not for that reason stop being _____ of the _____. *16* And if the ear should say, "Because I am not an eye, I do not belong to the _____," it would not for that reason stop being _____ of the _____. *17* If the whole _____ were an eye, where would the sense of hearing be? If the whole _____ were an ear, where would the sense of smell be? *18* But in fact God has placed the parts in the _____, every one of them, just as he wanted them to be. *19* If they were all one _____, where would the _____ be? *20* As it is, there are many _____, but one _____.

Based on the words used to fill in the blanks, what common terms or phrases do you see in these Scripture passages?

_____

_____

What kind of body or bodies is Paul referring to in these verses?

_____

_____

_____

Two are better than one, because they have a good return for their labor.

ECCLESIASTES 4:9

It's essential for the church to recognize itself as a community which works together for the common good of all. Paul compares this community to a human body whose movements, thoughts, and actions work together in unity. Just as a human body moves and thinks in a coordinated effort of many parts, so the body of Christ should live and move in a way in which each part functions for the good of all. Paul encourages the believers to recognize the importance of the gifts of others and work together in unity.

Do you think it's possible for different members of the body of Christ with varying gifts to work together in unity and purpose? Why or why not?

_____
_____
_____
_____
_____

According to H. C. G. Mounce, unity in diversity is possible within the church because all members are in Christ. Because the members are joined by faith and have become part of the body of Christ, each member belongs to all the others (Romans 12:5). Mounce believes Christian faith is essentially a corporate experience. Although each member comes to faith as a separate and individual act of faith, the body is a community that lives out its Christian experience in unity.[1]

Read Psalm 133.

What do these verses say about unity?

_____
_____
_____
_____
_____

Christians like snowflakes, are frail, but when they stick together they can stop traffic.
VANCE HAVNER

1. Mounce, *The New American Commentary: Romans*, 234.

According to Rick Warren, "Unity is the soul of fellowship. Destroy it, and you rip the heart out of Christ's body. It is the essence, the core, of how God intends for us to experience life together in his church."[2]

Is unity the same as uniformity? Does our oneness in Christ mean that we are not individuals? Why or why not?

_____

_____

_____

_____

_____

_____

Life Thoughts

While visiting my mother after surgery to have her appendix removed, I noticed a beautiful arrangement of flowers brought by one of the members of the church she attended. The flowers, she explained, were part of a sermon illustration given by the pastor in church that day.

During the sermon, after giving individual flowers to various members of the congregation, the pastor explained that the flowers represented the gifts God gives to us and that each flower is distinctly attractive in its own way. He later brought the flowers together as an example of the unity of the body of Christ—complementing and working together to make a beautiful bouquet.

---

2. Rick Warren, *The Purpose Driven Life* (Grand Rapids, MI: Zondervan, 2002), 160.

Are Some Members More Important Than Others?

Read 1 Corinthians 12:12–24.

What do these verses say about partiality in the body?

_____
_____
_____
_____
_____
_____

What do you think Paul means in verses 22–24 when he refers to some members of the body as being "weaker," "less honorable," or "unpresentable?" Is Paul saying that some members are not as important as others? Why or why not?

_____
_____
_____
_____
_____
_____
_____
_____

Life Scenario

Makena attends Eastside Community Church. She enjoys volunteering in church ministries and especially enjoys working in any areas that involve music. Makena is very talented in her musical abilities; she works with the church's audio system, mixing the music sung by the worship team, and working to help them to sound their best. Because Makena does not sing or play an instrument, however, she does not consider herself to be a part of the "worship team."

Chad, the church music director, has noticed that some of the worship team members are harsh at times with Makena, complaining if they think their microphones are not turned up loud enough, or if they think the other instruments are turned up too loud.

What do you think?

Do you think Makena should be considered a part of the worship team? Why or why not?

_____

_____

_____

_____

What might Chad say to encourage Makena in her ministry?

_____

_____

_____

_____

_____

How can the church show thankfulness to people like Makena whose jobs are less noticeable?

_____

_____

_____

_____

_____

Read 1 Corinthians 12:25–26.

Why does Paul say it is important to honor *all* members of the body?

_____

_____

_____

_____

_____

What does Paul mean by "suffering" with one another and "honoring" one another?

_____

_____

_____

_____

_____

_____

Can Chad do anything as the music director at Eastside Community Church to help the team work together better? If so, what might that be?

_____

_____

_____

_____

Life Thoughts

*I sometimes feel sorry for the worship team who is often held respon-
sible for whether or not "God's presence" is felt in a worship service.
Although it is true that the worship team is often instrumental in usher-
ing the body into God's presence, we as individual members must make
an effort to ensure that the "presence" remains. How often we complain
that the music is too loud or that something is distracting—this one is
out of tune—that one has no tune at all. Perhaps if we would remember*

to embrace this special time in our church service with an attitude of personal worship, we would realize that worship is a condition of the heart and that the tuneless song of the tin ear might actually be the joyful noise that God loves and honors.

In the following Scripture passages, what does Paul say about attitudes of superiority in the body of Christ?

Romans 12:3–5

_____

_____

_____

_____

_____

Ephesians 4:1–3

_____

_____

_____

_____

_____

How far you go in life depends on your being tender with the young, compassionate with the aged, sympathetic with the striving and tolerant of the weak and strong. Because someday in your life you will have been all of these.

GEORGE WASHINGTON CARVER

As parts of the body of Christ, Paul considered all members to be equal. In 1 Corinthians 12:13 he says we are all one body and that there is neither Jew nor Greek, slave or free. The body of Christ regards no socioeconomic status, no degrees based on intelligence—no partiality. As we humble ourselves in the eyes of God, we become lower in estate and more dependent on the gifts of others. The eye can never say to the hand, I don't need you, nor the head to the feet (1 Corinthians 12:21). More honor is given to the part that lacks (1 Corinthians 12:26).

Leith Anderson, author of *Leadership That Works; Hope and Direction for Church and Parachurch Leaders in Today's Complex World*, says, "First Corinthians 12 clearly teaches that we all have different gifts. Just as it is inappropriate for the foot to want to see or the eye to want to talk, it is inappropriate for us to wish we had someone else's spiritual gifts. It is the job of the Holy Spirit to distribute gifts and it is our job to be faithful stewards of the gifts we receive. To know and accept who we are, how we are gifted, and what God has called us to do is truly liberating. Then we can rejoice in God's gifts to others and be content with who we are."[3]

What problems might arise in a church fellowship where there are attitudes of superiority and inappropriate use of gifts?

_____

_____

_____

_____

_____

_____

_____

What can you do to encourage unity within your church fellowship?

_____

_____

_____

_____

_____

_____

---

3. Leith Anderson, _Leadership That Works; Hope and Direction for Church and Parachurch Leaders in Today's Complex World_ (Minneapolis: Bethany House Publishers, 1999), 173.

Self-Checklist

Read the following Scripture verses from Paul's teachings in Ephesians 4, Romans 12, and 1 Corinthians 12 concerning unity and the appropriate use of gifts. Answer the questions that relate to the verses indicated by rating yourself on a scale of 1 to 5 with the number 5 being yes, very much, and 1 being no, not at all.

1 Corinthians 12:13 *For we were all baptized by one Spirit so as to form one body—whether Jews or Gentiles, slave or free and we were all given the one Spirit to drink.*

Do you recognize the equality of those of other races and social status? 1 2 3 4 5

I Corinthians 12:15 *If the foot should say, "Because I am not a hand, I do not belong to the body," it would not for that reason cease to be part of the body.*

Do you recognize equality in the gifts of the body of Christ? 1 2 3 4 5

1 Corinthians 12:21 *The eye cannot say to the hand, "I don't need you!" And the head cannot say to the feet, "I don't need you!"*

Do you ask for help from others? 1 2 3 4 5

When supervising others, do you delegate authority to those members that are qualified? 1 2 3 4 5

1 Corinthians 12:22-23 *On the contrary, those parts of the body that seem to be weaker are indispensable, and the parts that we think are less honorable we treat with special honor.*

Do you give honor to the accomplishments of others? 1 2 3 4 5

1 Corinthians 12:26 *If one part suffers, every part suffers with it; if one part is honored, every part rejoices with it.*

Do you feel the pain of other Christians when they are hurting?

                            1 2 3 4 5

Do you rejoice rather than feel jealousy when other Christians are honored?

                            1 2 3 4 5

Romans 12:10 *Be devoted to one another in love. Honor one another above yourselves.*

Are you devoted to others in love?   1 2 3 4 5

Do you honor others above yourself?   1 2 3 4 5

Romans 12:13 *Share with the Lord's people who are in need. Practice hospitality.*

Do you help others in need?   1 2 3 4 5

Ephesians 4:2 *Be completely humble and gentle; be patient, bearing with one another in love.*

Are you humble and gentle in your attitude toward others?

                            1 2 3 4 5

At which of these "unity" character traits are you must successful?

_____

_____

_____

_____

Which of these unity character traits might need to be strengthened in your life?

_____

_____

_____

Jesus's Prayer of Unity

John 17:20–23

20 My prayer is not for them alone. I pray also for those who will believe in me through their message, 21 that all of them may be one, Father, just as you are in me and I am in you. May they also be in us so that the world may believe that you have sent me. 22 I have given them the glory that you gave me, that they may be one as we are one—23 I in them and you in me—so that they be brought to complete unity. Then the world will know that you sent me and have loved them even as you have loved me.

Write a prayer asking God to reveal his purposes in your church fellowship and how you can be used as an instrument to help promote unity.

Lord, I pray...

_____

_____

_____

_____

_____

_____

_____

_____

_____

_____

Lesson Ten
The Practice of Gifts

In a morally corrupt society, such as that of the Corinthian church, the concept of love was often mixed up or had little value. Therefore, after more fully instructing the Corinthians on the proper use of gifts and their importance in the body of Christ in 1 Corinthians 12, and before giving practical instruction as to their usage in the corporate worship setting in 1 Corinthians 14, Paul gave pause in his teaching to stress the importance of love.

In chapter 13, Paul portrays love as the key to the proper administration and practice of all gifts, and stresses the importance of its presence in the work of the church. To Paul, love is more important than any gift and is the catalyst behind the working of the body in unity. He refers to it as "the most excellent way" (1 Corinthians 12:31).

Read 1 Corinthians 13:1–3.

Fill in the blanks in the following passage:

> ¹ If I speak in the tongues of men or of angels, but do not have love, I am only a _____ _____ or a _____ _____
> _____. ² If I have the gift of prophecy and can fathom all mysteries and all knowledge, and if I have a faith that can move mountains, but do not have love, I am _____. ³ If I give all I possess to the poor and give over my body to hardship that I may boast, but do not have love, I gain _____.

Highlight or circle any gifts you see in the above passage.

What does Paul say in this Scripture passage about the relationship between gifts and love?

_____

_____

_____

It is the governing love of our Father and the loving hands of our brothers and sisters, reaching out to us—that serve as his answer in our hardest times.
DAVID WILKERSON

Why might Paul have compared the act of speaking with tongues without love to a "resounding gong" or a "clanging symbol," or as being "nothing"?

_____

_____

_____

_____

Life Thoughts

A child is not born speaking, nor do his or her parents teach the art of language by rehearsing a list of vocabulary words taken from a textbook. A child learns to communicate by listening and observing the communication of others. Word definitions are made known not only in spoken words, but in feelings, thoughts, and actions. This is especially true when a child is taught the meaning of the word love. If the concept is accompanied by gruff words and harsh actions, the child will have a different understanding than one who is told he or she is loved while receiving a hug.

So it is with God's children. God's love is taught by experiencing Him—a gentle voice, a kind embrace, and sometimes even a rod of discipline. As we continue in God's love, we will communicate the true meaning to others, not as a harsh and clanging cymbal, but in words that hug and embrace others, communicating not just in words, but in actions.

Doing doesn't count, unless Love motivates it; Love doesn't count unless doing demonstrates it.
WAYNE AND DIANE TESCH

What does Paul have to say about love and its relationship to gifts and unity in his other teachings on gifts in Romans 12 and Ephesians 4?

Romans 12:9–10

_____

_____

_____

_____

Ephesians 4:1–2

_____
_____
_____
_____

Ephesians 4:11–16

_____
_____
_____
_____

In his classic meditation *The Greatest Thing in the World*, Henry Drummond comments on the apostle Paul and his concept of love: "A man is apt to recommend to others his own strong point. Love was not Paul's strong point. The observing student can detect a beautiful tenderness growing and ripening all through his character as Paul gets old; but the hand that wrote, 'The greatest of these is love,' when we meet it first, is stained with blood."[1]

Because Paul, with his now blood-washed hands, mentions the significance of love in conjunction with our God-given gifts and the body of Christ in all three of his gift references in Romans, 1 Corinthians, and Ephesians, it is evident that he not only embraces the significance of love in regards to the church, but also has come to realize its absolute necessity.

Is love a gift or fruit of the Spirit (Galatians 5:22–23)?

_____
_____
_____

Dear friends, let us love one another, for love comes from God. Everyone who loves has been born of God and knows God. Whoever does not love does not know God, because God is love.
1 JOHN 4:7–8

---

1. Henry Drummond, *The Greatest Thing in the World* (Uhrichsville, OH: Barbour and Company, Inc. 1993), 8.

Read Christ's words in Matthew 22:34–40.

Why might Christ have put a greater emphasis on loving God and loving others than on the other commandments?

_____

_____

_____

_____

_____

_____

Read Romans 13: 8–10.

What do you think that Paul is referring to when he says that "love is the fulfillment of the law"?

_____

_____

_____

_____

_____

_____

In referring to Paul's words in this Scripture passage, Henry Drummond comments:

> "Did you ever think what he meant by that? In those days men were working their passage to Heaven by keeping the Ten Commandments, and the hundred and ten other commandments which they had manufactured out of them. Christ said, I will show you a more simple way. If you do one thing, you will do these hundred and ten things, without ever thinking about them. If you love, you will unconsciously fulfill the whole law. And you can readily see for yourselves how that must be so. Take any of the commandments, 'Thou shalt have no other gods before Me.' If a man love God, you will not require to tell him that. Love is the fulfilling of that law.... And so, if he loved Man, you would never think of telling him to honour his father and mother. He could not do anything

else. It would be preposterous to tell him not to kill…. In this way 'Love is the fulfilling of the law.' It is the rule for fulfilling all rules, the new commandment for keeping all the old commandments, Christ's one secret of the Christian life."[2]

Life Scenario

Just before Christmas every year, a local elementary school participated in what became known as "Santa's Workshop." The activity allowed the children from the school to do their own Christmas shopping for family members and friends. The store consisted of various items from which the students could purchase their presents. The children that participated brought a list of those persons for whom they wished to buy presents, along with their money. Volunteers helped the students purchase their gifts.

One particular boy spent a great deal of time selecting gifts for his family. He put a lot of thought into the purchases and tried hard to use all his money for his family. Several times he was disappointed that he did not have enough money for a certain present. Another boy tried to buy the cheapest gifts possible for his family members so that he would have as much money as possible left over to buy something for himself. Both boys used all their money, but in different ways.

It is not how much you do, but how much love you put into the doing that matters.
MOTHER TERESA

What difference do you see in the attitudes of the two boys?

_____

_____

_____

_____

Circle or highlight the attributes of love that Paul mentions in the following Scripture passages concerning gifts and unity.

1 Corinthians 13:4–7

4 Love is patient, love is kind. It does not envy, it does not boast, it is not proud. 5 It does not dishonor others, it is not self-seeking, it is not eas-

---

2. Drummond, *The Greatest Thing in the World*, 8–9.

ily angered, it keeps no record of wrongs. ⁶ Love does not delight in evil but rejoices with the truth. ⁷ It always protects, always trusts, always hopes, always perseveres.

Romans 12:9

⁹ Love must be sincere. Hate what is evil; cling to what is good.

Life Thoughts

Howard, excited to visit his wife of seventy-one years, was even more excited that we were accompanying him to the nursing home. Nettie didn't get many visitors.

Needless to say, Howard was more eager than I was. Not caring much for nursing homes, I always try to prepare myself upon entering a facility. Scenes of grown women cradling baby dolls and despondent faces never cease to overwhelm me. Howard, however, did not seem to notice. He proudly led us down the hall to his wife's room as we dodged wheelchairs, saying hello to faces that reflected a mixture of smiles and sadness.

Things didn't get much better when we entered the room. Nettie had no idea who we were. Howard explained that he was the only one she recognized anymore. Judging from the blank look on her face, I secretly wondered if she sometimes did not even recognize him. I settled in a chair for what I hoped would not be too long a visit.

Nettie couldn't speak much but followed us with her eyes and occasionally smiled. She was completely bedridden and very thin. We watched as Howard took her liquid diet and patiently coaxed her to take each mouthful. The feeding took forty-five minutes, throughout which time he excitedly told us stories of their life. They had eloped when they were seventeen...soon they would both be eight-nine. Howard told of their times working together in the ministry, tales we had heard before, but always made me smile.

The stories were not what captivated me this particular day however; today I was witnessing a drama, a beautiful love story. I watched Howard croon to his wife and kiss her, comb her hair, and tell her of his love.

We left the nursing home with a new appreciation of love, marriage, and each other. I knew that I had witnessed a very special thing, a story that would continue through eternity—a portrait of love, the God kind.

Read 1 Corinthians 13:8–13.

How is love different from prophecy, tongues, and knowledge?

_____

_____

_____

_____

_____

In verse 13, Paul says that faith, hope, and love remain, but the greatest of these is love.

Why might Paul have said that the greatest of these three is love?

_____

_____

_____

_____

Love Checklist

Read the following Scripture verses from Paul's teachings in Romans 12, 1 Corinthians 12, and Ephesians 4 concerning love. Answer the questions that relate to the verses indicated by rating yourself on a scale of 1 to 5 with the number 5 being yes, very much, and 1 being no, not at all.

1 Corinthians 13:4 *Love is patient, love is kind. It does not envy, it does not boast, it is not proud.*

I tend to have great patience with people, even when they display repeated failures.　　　　　　　　　　　　**1　2　3　4　5**

I am generally kind to people even when they are harsh or show anger toward me.   1 2 3 4 5

I am happy for others who receive rewards or recognition even when I do not receive recognition myself.   1 2 3 4 5

I do not generally display boastfulness or become prideful in my accomplishments.   1 2 3 4 5

> **1 Corinthians 13:5** *[Love] does not dishonor others, it is not self-seeking, it is not easily angered, it keeps no record of wrongs.*

I am courteous and usually allow others to go first.   1 2 3 4 5

I seek the good of others before my own good.   1 2 3 4 5

I am not easily angered.   1 2 3 4 5

I forgive easily.   1 2 3 4 5

> **1 Corinthians 13:6–7** *⁶ Love does not delight in evil but rejoices with the truth. ⁷ It always protects, always trusts, always hopes, always perseveres.*

I am sad when people are hurting, even when they "get what they deserve."   1 2 3 4 5

I am protective of the interests and feelings of others. 1 2 3 4 5

I am trustful of others.   1 2 3 4 5

I generally hope for the best.   1 2 3 4 5

I persevere in what I know to be right.   1 2 3 4 5

Romans 12:9 *Love must be sincere. Hate what is evil; cling to what is good.*

I am sincere in my expressions of love to others.   1   2   3   4   5

I am disturbed by what is evil.   1   2   3   4   5

I follow after that which is good.   1   2   3   4   5

Ephesians 4:15 *Speaking the truth in love, we will grow to become in every respect the mature body of him who is the head, that is, Christ.*

I speak the truth of God's Word in love.   1   2   3   4   5

At which of these love attributes are you must successful?

_____

_____

_____

Which love attributes may need to be strengthened in your life?

_____

_____

_____

Alan F. Johnson says, "the language of 1 Corinthians 13 has found a way into the church's marriage liturgy, sermons, hymns and every Christian's heart as the most profound description of the kind of love expressed through Jesus Christ toward us, as well as in the life of his servant, Paul."[3]

Paul recognized that not only is love vital to the proper functioning of the church, but that without it all the efforts of the body are useless. Love is the enduring concept that will function throughout eternity. It is the spiritual center of the church.

---

3. Alan F. Johnson, *The IVP New Testament Commentary Series: 1 Corinthians* Series Eds. Grant R. Osborne, D. Stuart Briscoe, and Haddon Robinson. (Downers Grove, IL: Inter-Varsity Press, 2004), 240.

Life Thoughts

The God of Christianity is a God who loves unconditionally regardless of our actions. Unlike other religions, God's love is not based on what is received or will be received from the beloved. We are loved not because of our works or how deserving we are—not because of how much we love, or how good we love, but because God is love.

What things can you do to help ensure that you are using your God-given gifts within the context of love?

_____

_____

_____

_____

Conclusion

The subject of gifts continues to be a topic of great controversy. I pray that this study has helped you to define, or at least come closer to defining, your own personal definition of what gifts are, as well as to help you more fully understand and appreciate the views of others. Despite our varying opinions, we are the body of Christ which is joined together in unity and love.

Think back over all you have learned in the past weeks of this study. Write your own definition of gifts. Explain how they should be used in ministry.

_____

_____

_____

_____

_____

_____

_____

_____

Our challenge today is not only to understand the purpose and practice of God's gifts to His people, but to begin recognizing our own unique gifts, as well as those of our fellow Christians. In this way we can work together effectively as the body that God created us to be, without partiality and without hypocrisy, in our efforts to fulfill the great commission of reaching the world for Christ. In Romans 10:14 Paul asks,

"How, then, can they call on the one they have not believed in? And how can they believe in the one of whom they have not heard? And how can they hear without someone preaching to them?"

Along with Paul's questions, we too might ask: How can we, as the body of Christ, hear if we have no ears? How can we see if we have no eyes? And how can we touch others without the hands of the body extended to the world? All of which is to be done, as Paul reminds us, in the context of *love*, because without *love*, we are nothing (1 Corinthians 13:2).

I pray that just as the apostle Paul admonished the workings of the body to be done in love that we would continue to remember that without it we are nothing.

Hebrews 13:20–21

²⁰ Now may the God of peace, who through the blood of the eternal covenant brought back from the dead our Lord Jesus, that great Shepherd of the sheep, ²¹ equip you with everything good for doing his will, and may he work in us what is pleasing to him, through Jesus Christ, to whom be glory for ever and ever. Amen.

*Hast thou not seen
how thy desires
e'er have been
granted in what
He ordaineth?*
PRAISE YE THE LORD,
THE ALMIGHTY (HYMN)
JOACHIM NEANDER

153

Write a prayer that God will help you to understand and use the gifts He has given you as well as more fully understanding the gifts of others.

Lord I pray...

_____

_____

_____

_____

_____

_____

_____

_____

_____

_____

_____

May God richly bless you in His kingdom work.

BIBLIOGRAPHY

Aker, Benny C. "Charismata: Gifts, Enablements, or Ministries." *Journal of Pentecostal Theology* vol. 11, no. 1 (Oct 2002): 54–69.

Aker, Benny C. and Gary B. McGee, eds. *Signs and Wonders in Ministry Today.* Springfield, MO: Gospel Publishing House, 1996.

Anderson, Leith. *Leadership That Works; Hope and Direction for Church and Parachurch Leaders in Today's Complex World.* Minneapolis: Bethany House Publishers, 1999.

Arnold, Clinton E. *Ephesians: Power and Magic The Concept of Power in Ephesians in Light of its Historical Setting.* New York: Cambridge University Press, 1989.

Arrington, French L. and Roger Stronstad, eds. *Full Life Bible Commentary to the New Testament.* Grand Rapids, MI: Zondervan Publishing House, 1999.

Barclay, William. *The Letters to the Galatians and Ephesians.* rev. ed. Philadelphia: The Westminster Press, 1977.

Barram, Michael D. "Romans 12:9–21." *Interpretation* vol. 57, no. 4 (2003): 423–426.

Berkhof, Louis. *Systematic Theology.* Grand Rapids, MI: William B. Eerdmans, 1996.

Bernard, David K. *Spiritual Gifts: A Practical Study with Inspirational Accounts of God's Supernatural Gifts to His Church.* Hazelwood, MO: Word Aflame Press, 1956.

Black, Matthew. *The New Century Bible Commentary: Romans.* 2nd ed. Grand Rapids, MI: William B. Eerdmans, 1989.

Bloesch, Donald G. *Essentials of Evangelical Theology, 2 Volumes in One.* San Francisco: Prince Press-Harper Collins, 2006.

Brown, Colin, ed. *The New International Dictionary of New Testament Theology.* Grand Rapids, MI: Zondervan Publishing House, 1971.

Bible.org. Boa, Kenneth. "The Gifts of the Spirit." http://bible.org/article/gifts-spirit (accessed June 24, 2009).

Bible.org. Keathley, J. Hampton III. "The Stewardship of Talents." http://bible.org/seriespage/stewardship-talents (accessed June, 24, 2009).

Bonnke, Reinhard. *Mighty Manifestations; the Gifts and Power of the Holy Spirit.* rev. ed. Frankfort, Germany: Full Flame GmbH, 2002.

Brandt, R. L. *Gifts for the Marketplace.* Tulsa: Christian Publishing Services, Inc., 1989.

Bridges, James K., ed. *Pentecostal Gifts and Ministries in a Postmodern Era.* Springfield, MO: Gospel Publishing, 2004.

Bryant, Charles V. *Rediscovering Our Spiritual Gifts: Building Up the Body of Christ Through the Gifts of the Spirit.* 6th ed. Nashville: Upper Room Books, 1991.

Bullock, Warren D. *When the Spirit Speaks.* Springfield, MO: Gospel Publishing House, 2009.

Carson, D. A. *Showing the Spirit: A Theological Exposition of 1 Corinthians 12–14.* Grand Rapids, MI: Baker Books, 1987.

Drummond, Henry. *The Greatest Thing in the World.* Uhrichsville, OH: Barbour and Company, Inc., 1993.

Elbert, Paul. "Calvin and the Spiritual Gifts." *Journal of the Evangelical Theological Society* vol. 22, no. 3 (Sept. 1979): 235–256.

Fee, Gordon D. *The First Epistle to the Corinthians.* Grand Rapids, MI: William B. Eerdmans Publishing Company, 1987.

Fee, Gordon D. and Stuart, Douglas. *How to Read the Bible for All Its Worth.* 3rd ed. Grand Rapids, MI: Zondervan, 2003.

Fitzmyer, Joseph A. *First Corinthians: A New Translation with Introduction and Commentary* vol. 32, in The Anchor Bible, USA: Yale University Press, 2008.

Fitzmyer, Joseph A. *Romans: A New Translation with Introduction and Commentary.* vol. 33, in *The Anchor Bible*, New York, NY: Doubleday, 1993.

Flynn, Leslie B. *19 Gifts of the Spirit,* Wheaton: Victor Books, A division of SP Publications, 1975.

Foster, Richard. *Celebration of Discipline.* San Francisco: Harper Collins Publisher, 1998.

Gaffin, Richard B. Jr. *Perspectives on Pentecost.* Grand Rapids, MI: Baker Book House, 1979.

Gee, Donald. *Concerning Spiritual Gifts.* rev. ed. Springfield, MO: Gospel Publishing House, 1972.

Grossmann, Siegfried. *There Are Other Gifts than Tongues,* trans. by Susan Wiesmann, Wheaton: Tyndale House publishers, 1971.

Grudem, Wayne, ed. *Are Miraculous Gifts for Today: Four Views.* Grand Rapids, MI: Zondervan Publishing House, 1996.

Gundry, Robert H. *A Survey of the New Testament*. Grand Rapids: Zondervan Publishing House, 1994.

Guthrie, Donald. *Exploring God's Word: A Guide to Ephesians, Philippians, and Colossians*. 1984. rep., Grand Rapids, MI: William B. Eerdmans Publishing Company, 1985.

Guthrie, Donald. *New Testament Introduction*. 3rd. Downers Grove, IL: InterVarsity Press, 1970.

Hayes, John H. ed. *1 Corinthians, 2 Corinthians / William Baird. Knox Preaching Guides*. Atlanta: John Knox Press, 1980.

Hayford, Jack W. ed. With Gary Matsdorf, *People of the Spirit: Gifts, Fruit and Fullness of the Holy Spirit*. Nashville: Thomas Nelson Publishers, 1993.

Hodge, Charles. *A Commentary on 1 & 2 Corinthians*. 1857. Reprint, Carlisle, PA: The Banner of Truth Trust, 1983.

Horton, Stanley M. *1 & 2 Corinthians: A Logion Press Commentary*. Springfield, MO: Gospel Publishing, 1999.

House, Wayne H. *Charts of Christian Theology & Doctrine*. Grand Rapids, MI: Zondervan, 1992.

Hubbard, David Allen. *Unwrapping Your Spiritual Gifts*. Waco, TX: Word Books Pub., 1985.

Hughes, R. Kent. *The Mystery of the Body of Christ*. Wheaton, IL: Crossway Books, 1990.

Hurst, Randy, ed., *Divine Order: Leading the Public Use of Spiritual Gifts*. Access Group for Gospel Publishing House, 2009.

Jamieson, Faussett Commentary. http://eword.gospelcom.net/comments/romans/jfb/romans12.htm (accessed August 30, 2008).

Johnson, Alan F. *The IVP New Testament Commentary Series: 1 Corinthians. Series* Eds. Grant R. Osborne, D. Stuart Briscoe, and Haddon Robinson. Downers Grove, IL: InterVarsity Press, 2004.

Keener, Craig S. *Gift & Giver: The Holy Spirit for Today*. Grand Rapids, MI: Baker Academic, 2001.

Lee, Edgar R., ed. *He Gave Apostles: Apostolic Ministry in the 21st Century*. Springfield, MO: Assemblies of God Theological Seminary, 2005.

Lim, David. *Spiritual Gifts: A Fresh Look*. Springfield, MO: Gospel Publishing House, 1991.

Macchia, Frank D. *Baptized in the Spirit: A Global Pentecostal Theology*. Grand Rapids, MI: Zondervan, 2006.

Malphurs, Aubrey. *Maximizing Your Effectiveness: How to Discover and Develop Your Divine Design*. 2nd ed. Grand Rapids, MI: Baker Books, 2006.

Matthew Henry Commentary. http://www.biblegateway.com/resources/commentaries/index.php?action=getBookSections&cid=33&source=2(accessed September 11, 2008).

Moule, H. C. G. *Ephesians Studies*. Fort Washington, PA: Christian Literature Crusade, 1937.

Mounce, Robert H. ed., *The New American Commentary: An Exegetical and Theological Exposition of Holy Scripture, Romans*. vol. 27, USA: Broadman & Holman Publishers, 1995.

Myra H., & Shelley, M. *The Leadership Secrets of Billy Graham*. Grand Rapids, MI: Zondervan, 2005.

Nelson's Complete Book of Bible Maps and Charts. Nashville: Thomas Nelson Publishers, 1996.

Osborne, Grant R. *The Hermeneutical Spiral*. Downers Grove, IL: InterVarsity Press, 2006.

Packer, James I. "Experiencing God's Presents: is Every Believer Guaranteed at Least One Spiritual Gift?" *Christianity Today* vol. 47, no. 8 (August 2003): 55–56.

Palma, Anthony D. "Spiritual Gifts—Basic Considerations," *Pneuma* vol. 1, no 2 (Fall 1979): 3–26.

Pearlman, Myer. *Knowing the Doctrines of the Bible*. Springfield, MO: Gospel Publishing House, 1937.

Prior, David. *The Message of 1 Corinthians: Life in the Local Church*. Downers Grove, IL: InterVarsity Press, 1985.

Rees, Erik. *S.H.A.P.E.* Grand Rapids, MI: Zondervan, 2006.

Schwarz, Christian A. *The 3 Colors of Ministry*. St. Charles, IL: ChurchSmart Resources, 2001.

Stitzinger, James F. "Spiritual Gifts: Definitions and Kinds." *Master's Seminary Journal* vol. 14, no. 2 (2003): 143-176.

Stott, John R. W. *The Message of Ephesians*. Downers Grove, IL: InterVarsity Press, 1979.

Tenney, Merrill C. *New Testament Survey*. rev. ed. Grand Rapids, MI: William B. Eerdmans, 1985.

Tenney, Merrill C. *New Testament Times*. Grand Rapids, MI: William B. Eerdmans, 1965.

Turner, Max. *The Holy Spirit and Spiritual Gifts: in the New Testament Church and Today*. rev. ed. Peabody, MA: Hendrickson, 1998.

Wagner, C. Peter. *The Third Wave of the Holy Spirit*. Ann Arbor, MI: Vine Books Servant Publications, 1988.

Wagner, C. Peter. *Your Spiritual Gifts Can Help Your Church Grow*. Glendale, CA: GL Regal Books Division/ GL Publications, 1980.

Walvoord, John F. "The Holy Spirit and Spiritual Gifts" *Bibliotheca sacra* vol. 143, no. 560 (Ap-Je 1986): 109–122.

Warfield, Benjamin B. *Counterfeit Miracles*. 1918 Reprint, London: The Banner of Truth Trust, 1972.

Warren, Rick. *The Purpose Driven Life*. Grand Rapids, MI: Zondervan, 2002.

Yong, Amos. "Discerning the Spirit." *Christian Century* vol. 123, no. 5 (March 7, 2006): 3–26.

Yong, Amos. *The Spirit Poured Out on All Flesh: Pentecostalism and the Possibility of Global Theology*. Grand Rapids, MI: Baker Academic, 2005.

WHAT ARE SPIRITUAL GIFTS?
How to Decide When Even the Experts Disagree

C. A. PATRICK

Leaders' Guide
Course Purpose and Objectives

Thank you for agreeing to be a leader in this study. Be assured that your role is very important. Not only will you be instrumental in making sure sessions are completed in a timely and efficient manner, but you will have the opportunity to display the love of Christ to others. At times you might feel you are not up to the task. In these times remember, "it is God who works in you to will and to act in order to fulfill his good purpose" (Philippians 2:13). I pray God will bless as you willingly serve God and others.

The purpose of this Bible study is to allow participants to develop their own definition of spiritual gifts using interactive, facilitative Bible study methods. In this study, participants will discuss biblical concepts of spiritual gifts using the apostle Paul's gift list passages in Romans 12, 1 Corinthians 12–14, and Ephesians 4, as well as interacting with various scholarly resources. The Leaders' Guide is designed to prepare and equip group overseers and facilitators to implement this Bible study curriculum.

Course Overview

This study is designed to be completed over the course of eleven weeks in once-a-week sessions. Depending on the size of your group, a group overseer might be needed—one person who will act as the overall coordinator and organizer. You will also need facilitators (ideally one person for up to eight people) who are responsible for keeping lessons on track and encouraging group members in their personal study of God's Word. The Introductory Session is a combined group session led by the group overseer and facilitators. The session will include a course introduction, small group covenant, and a short time of group interaction. Lessons One through Ten will be conducted by group facilitators and will involve prior homework preparation by participants and substantial small group interaction during study sessions.

Participant Preparation

The purpose of any Bible study should be to encourage participants in their Christian growth by providing them with a means of studying Scripture while stimulating a hunger to understand and apply the Word of God to their personal lives. During the Introductory Session, participants will be given a workbook with reading assignments and activities which should be completed prior to the sessions over the course of the next ten weeks. These lessons are designed to familiarize them with the subject matter so they are prepared to interact when the group meets. This format should allow for discussion and enable participants to learn from other group members concerning principles encountered during individual personal studies throughout the week.

General Responsibilities of Participants

- Arrive on time

- Complete homework assignments prior to sessions

- Come prepared to engage in small group discussions

- Abide by the small group covenant agreement as outlined in the Introductory Session

Facilitator Preparation

Small group facilitators will guide discussions of each week's Bible studies and applications. Facilitators may be given freedom in formatting discussions, but should allow for maximum participation by individual group members. Facilitators will use the same workbook as participants with no additional information other than the basic course information found in the Leaders' Guide. During group sessions, facilitators will continue to keep discussions focused and on task, but will also become active members in the learning process.

General Responsibilities of Facilitators

- Pray for Holy Spirit guidance

- Keep a humble spirit

- Be enthusiastic

- Open with prayer (if prayer requests are given, make sure requests are brief)

- Keep discussion focused and on task

- Encourage participation by all members

- Discourage monopolization of conversation by one or more members

- Be prepared and encourage other group members to be prepared

- Maintain guidelines of the established group covenant as outlined in the Introductory Session

- Become personally involved without relinquishing leadership role

- Allow for a break if needed

- End sessions on time

Group Overseer Preparation

The group overseer is responsible for the Introductory Session and, if needed, any brief opening remarks for Lessons One through Ten. In the Introductory Session, the group overseer will introduce the study and discuss the small group covenant. After explaining these basics, the overseer should allow students to break into small groups for a short time of interactive discussion. The Introductory Session Group Discussion Questions, provided with this study, may be used for this portion of the session. Please leave ample time for this important part of the Introductory Session. It will give participants a taste of what is ahead and will help them become acquainted with the people they will be interacting with during the weeks ahead. Group overseers may join a study group for the remainder of the sessions as a *participant only*.

General Responsibilities of Group Overseer

- Pray for Holy Spirit guidance

- Keep a humble spirit

- Be enthusiastic

- Oversee Introductory Session

- Assist group facilitators when needed

- Be familiar with the course material

- Help to enforce guidelines established in group covenants

Leaders' Guide
Course Content

Introductory Session

This session will introduce the subject of spiritual gifts and their importance in ministry, as well as giving a general idea of the controversy and problems involving the definition of spiritual gifts.

Lesson One • The Early Church

In this lesson, participants will study the historical context of the scriptural passages concerning gifts in Romans, 1 Corinthians, and Ephesians. This is an important step in the studying of the Bible people very often miss. Discovering how people lived during the time of the early church, and exploring the reasons why the subject of gifts was addressed in the manner in which it was, is a process that can be new and exciting to those who have never studied in this way. Comparing what they did then and what we do now can also be fun.

Lesson Two • Grace Gifts: Natural or Supernatural?

In this session, the theme for Paul's gift passages will be introduced and the Greek terminology for gifts, *charismata*, and their relationship to grace, *charis*, will be discussed. There will also be discussion outlining the controversy involved in whether or not the gifts were intended to be natural, supernatural, or a combination of both.

Lesson Three • The Romans Gift List

This lesson will discuss the varying definitions of the gifts in the Romans gift list, allowing participants to interact with various scholarly resources in an effort to write their own definitions of the gifts in this Scripture passage.

Lesson Four • The Corinthians 12:8–10 Gift List

This lesson will allow for interaction with the 1 Corinthians 12:8–10 gift list and definitions from biblical sources as well as various scholarly resources. As in Lesson Three, participants will attempt to write their own definitions of these New Testament gifts.

Lesson Five • Are All Gifts for Today?

In this lesson, participants will discuss the various ideas of the Cessationist, Pentecostal, Charismatic, and Third Wave movements, addressing the question of whether or not all the gifts in the apostle Paul's gift lists should be active in today's church. The session will be completed by discussing the remaining gifts in 1 Corinthians 12:28–30.

Lesson Six • The Ephesians Gift List

Lesson Six involves more interaction with Scripture and scholarly resources involving the definition of the Ephesians gift list. Participants will continue to write their own definitions concerning these gifts.

Lesson Seven • Questions Concerning Gifts

Lesson Seven will involve the question debated among Christians as to whether or not there are other gifts besides those mentioned by the apostle Paul in Scripture. There will also be discussion as to the Trinitarian source of gifts and the problems concerning false gifts.

Lesson Eight • What Gifts Are Not

This lesson explores topics involving the confusion surrounding the definition and purpose of gifts by analyzing what the gifts are not. Focus will be directed toward the difference between the fruit of the Spirit and the gifts of the Spirit, and questions as to the difference between gifted individuals and the Christian's universal responsibilities.

Lesson Nine • The Purpose of Gifts

In this lesson there will be interaction between the Scripture passages involving Paul's three gift lists and various scholarly resources, in an effort to define the purpose of gifts for unity in ministry.

Lesson Ten • The Practice of Gifts

This lesson will involve the practice of gifts in what Paul defines as "the most excellent way"—in unity and love.

A Final Note to Overseers and Facilitators

Thank you for your willingness to participate in this Bible study as an overseer or facilitator. I pray as Paul did in Ephesians 3:16–19:

> [16] …that out of his glorious riches he may strengthen you with power through his Spirit in your inner being, [17] so that Christ may dwell in your hearts through faith. And I pray that you, being rooted and established in love, [18] may have power, together with all the Lord's holy people, to grasp how wide and long and high and deep is the love of Christ, [19] and to know this love that surpasses knowledge—that you may be filled to the measure of all the fullness of God.

God bless you.

Leaders' Guide
Introductory Session
Group Discussion Questions

Life Scenario

Dan is attending a small group Bible study for the first time. While introducing himself to the group, Dan comments that because he is a new Christian, he will not be participating in group discussions, but will only be listening to the comments of others.

How would you respond to Dan's comment?

_____

_____

_____

_____

Do you believe that Dan, as a new Christian, has anything to share that would be beneficial to someone who has been a Christian for a longer period of time? If so, what might that be?

_____

_____

_____

_____

Life Scenario

Alicia has been a Christian for two years. She has participated in several small group Bible studies and enjoys the group interaction. After learning that the current Bible study she planned to attend would be discussing the subject of Christian gifts, however, Alicia hesitated about joining the group. Alicia does not feel that she is gifted in any way. She feels that she is just an ordinary person who can help with the gifts of others, but does not have any significant gifts that would be of value to the church.

169

Do you believe it's possible that Alicia does not have any gifts? Why or why not?

_____

_____

_____

_____

How might you encourage Alicia to join the Bible study?

_____

_____

_____

_____

Leaders' Guide
Group Covenant

Before you begin the assignments, discuss the following guidelines for small group study with group members. Copies of the covenant for participants to sign are available at your discretion from the publisher's website, www.morningjoymedia.com/resources.

As a small group member I agree to do the following:

1. Come prepared to participate in studies by completing homework assignments to the best of my ability.

2. Be faithful in attendance as much as possible.

3. Participate in group discussions in a manner that brings honor to God and to other group members.

4. Encourage others as they seek and use their God-given gifts. Respect the opinions of others as fellow lifelong learners.

5. Give opportunity for all group members to participate. Keep comments short and to the point.

6. Stay focused on the planned lessons. Avoid veering off into other topics not related to the lessons.

7. Keep personal matters shared within the group setting confidential.

8. Recognize that my conclusions at the end of this study might not necessarily be the same as those of other group members.